LEVELS 15-20

Engage Literacy TEACHER'S RESOURCE

Orange, Turquoise and Purple

Lauren White

Engage Literacy is published in 2013 by Raintree.
Raintree is an imprint of Capstone Global Library Limited, a company incorporated in Engand and Wales having its registered office at 7 Pilgrim Street, London, EC4V 6LB – Registered company number: 6695582
www.raintreepublishers.co.uk

Originally published in Australia by Hinkler Education, a division of Hinkler Books Pty Ltd.
Text and illustrations copyright © Hinkler Books Pty Ltd 2012

Written by Lauren White
Lead authors Jay Dale and Anne Giulieri
Illustrations by Anna Hancock
Edited by Anne McKenna
UK edition edited by Dan Nunn, Sian Smith and Catherine Veitch
Designed by Susannah Low, Butterflyrocket Design
Typeset by Anne Stanhope

All rights reserved. No part of this publication may be reproduced, stored in a retrieval system, or transmitted in any way or by any means, electronic, mechanical, photocopying, recording or otherwise, without the prior written permission of Capstone Global Library Limited.

Engage Literacy Teacher's Resource Levels 15–20
Orange, Turquoise and Purple
ISBN: 978 1 406 26361 9
10 9 8 7 6 5 4 3 2 1

Printed and bound in China by Leo Paper Products Ltd

Acknowledgements
Cover photograph: © Brett Atkins | Dreamstime.com

Contents

Please note the following abbreviations that are used in the Teacher's Resource:

HFW: High-Frequency Words **PW:** Photocopiable Worksheet **ELL:** English Language Learners **IWB:** Interactive Whiteboard

Introduction

Engage Literacy is a comprehensive literacy programme that can be used with an individual, small-group and/or whole-class focus. The core elements of a balanced literacy programme have been covered, i.e. written language (reading and writing) and oral language (speaking and listening). The programme covers reading levels 1 to 25 (book bands Pink to Lime), and includes both fiction and non-fiction texts. Texts are curriculum-linked, and the Levels 2 to 25 fiction texts link thematically to corresponding non-fiction titles.

Engage Literacy brings enjoyment and humour to reading while providing teachers and children with carefully graded and levelled texts. Through engaging and high-interest fiction and non-fiction texts, rhymes, poems, songs and chants, children will become active participants in their own learning and in the reading process.

The *Engage Literacy* components provide both digital and non-digital teaching and learning materials that promote differentiated learning so all children can learn effectively, regardless of differences in ability levels. All components of the programme are built on a comprehensive scope and sequence document that covers essential literacy skills and knowledge, i.e. oral language, phonological awareness, text conventions, vocabulary, fluency, comprehension and writing. This scope and sequence document underpins all the components of *Engage Literacy,* including literacy assessment through Running Records. Teachers can be assured that by implementing *Engage Literacy* in their classrooms, their children's individual learning needs will be met effectively.

Engage Literacy components

- *Fiction and non-fiction texts for reading levels 1 to 25*
  All levelled texts, both fiction and non-fiction, have been developed using carefully graded vocabulary lists, e.g. the word 'go' is introduced at Level 1 and 'going' is introduced at Level 4. Children therefore build up a bank of high-frequency words, providing them with a smoother transition as they are introduced to higher-level texts. The texts enable children to build on their prior knowledge and make new connections based on these previous understandings. *Engage Literacy* also includes a progressive academic vocabulary list of words such as 'draw', 'make' and 'write', which are essential for early readers to successfully understand and complete academic tasks independently.

  Engage Literacy ensures that children are exposed to texts that match their developmental reading level, enabling greater potential for reading success and enhancing fluency. As they move through the levels in *Engage Literacy,* children will encounter words they have met in texts from the previous levels. The earlier levelled texts have a ratio of introduced words to known words of 1:20.

Reading stage	*Engage Literacy* reading level	Book band	Reading age (approx.)
Emergent	Levels 1–2	Pink	4½–6½ years
Emergent/Early	Levels 3–5	Red	
Early	Levels 6–8	Yellow	
Early	Levels 9–11	Blue	
Early/Fluent	Levels 12–14	Green	
Fluent	Levels 15–16	Orange	7 years
Fluent	Levels 17–18	Turquoise	7½ years
Fluent	Levels 19–20	Purple	8 years
Fluent	Levels 21–22	Gold	8½ years
Fluent	Levels 23–24	White	9 years
Fluent	Levels 25	Lime	9½ years

On the back of each fiction and non-fiction title, the reading stage is shown (e.g. Emergent/Early), as well as the specific graded level of the text (e.g. Level 4). Book band colour coding is also used to represent each level. The table on page iv shows an approximate correlation between the reading stage, reading level, book band colour and reading age.

All texts feature, on the inside front cover, information that enables the teacher to gain a quick overview of the text. See the example to the right.

Up and Down

Level 2 Fiction

Word count: 58

Curriculum link:
animals/minibeasts, science, environment

Text type: narrative

Sentence structure:
"I can go up/down," said the ______.

High-frequency words introduced:
and, can, down

High-frequency words consolidated:
go, I, said, the, up

Example inferential questions:
- *Why do you think the bird is going up?*
- *Why do you think the snail is going down?*

Phonological awareness:
initial letter sounds a, s, b, w, c

Linking texts:
Look at the Animals (NF)
Digital Poster 'Snail'

Above: Inside front cover

- *Teacher's Resource*
  Each title in *Engage Literacy* is accompanied by an extensive teacher's resource book that includes teaching notes, photocopiable worksheets and a Running Record for each title. See page vi for more information.

Above: Digital Poster

- *Digital Posters*
  The *Engage Literacy Digital Posters* can be used on individual computers and IWBs. They feature rhymes, poems, songs and chants that link to each fiction and non-fiction text at Levels 1 to 15. The posters can be used with the whole class or a small group, and encourage the development of speaking and listening skills through a shared learning experience.

Above: Oral Language Book A spread

- *Oral Language Big Books*
  These large-format books promote children's oral language and visual literacy skills. Extensive teaching notes have been provided, which include comprehensive question stems. English as a Second Language (ESL) students and English Language Learners (ELL) will benefit greatly from the vocabulary covered in these books.

- *Wonder Words pack*
  This pack helps children to learn their first 100 high-frequency words in context, through real stories. There are 24 fiction titles from levels 1 to 15 (book bands Pink to Orange), which use repetition, rhythm and common phrases to help children, particularly English Language Learners, to learn to read and recognise their first 100 essential words. An accompanying teacher's resource book, which includes an introduction and photocopiable pupil worksheets, is included in the pack.

Above: Wonder Words pack

Fiction and non-fiction texts

A balance of the following text forms and text types has been included in all texts over the 25 levels.

Fiction

Narrative: purpose—to entertain, e.g. ballad, poetry, personal recount, song, historical recount, fairy tale, myth

Non-fiction

Report: purpose—to provide information about a particular topic, e.g. report, descriptive report, investigative report, scientific/technical report, newspaper article, project, internet, thinking hats

Transactional: purpose—to communicate and clarify, e.g. survey, questionnaire, complaint, apology, greeting card, interview, introduction, invitation, letter, speech, email, newsletter

Recount: purpose—to retell an experience or an event, e.g. personal, factual, imaginative, biography, historical recount, autobiography

Procedural: purpose—to tell how to do something or to explain how to get somewhere, e.g. directions, instructions, message, agenda, recipe, manual, rules for game

Exposition (argument): purpose—to argue for one side of an issue, e.g. argument, speech, debate

Exposition (persuasive): purpose—to persuade or convince others, e.g. advertisement or commercial, cartoon, pamphlet

Explanation: purpose—to explain why or how things happen, e.g. scientific, technical, life, historical

Description: purpose—to detail the characteristics of a subject (using the five senses, similes and metaphors), e.g. poetry, descriptive recount, descriptive report, historical report, internet, police report

Discussion: purpose—to present different aspects of an issue, e.g. brochures, reports, current issues, class rules, reviews, newspapers, 'what ifs', PMIs (Pluses, Minuses, [New] Ideas)

Response: purpose—to give a personal response to something, e.g. book/film/art review, letter, diary

Teacher's Resource

Each *Teacher's Resource* provides comprehensive, easy-to-use teaching notes with accompanying photocopiable worksheets for each title. Each set of teaching notes provides:

- **Story or text summary**
- **Tuning in:** activities that 'tune in' students to the topic/s in the text
- **Book walk**: page-by-page questions and discussions to cue children into illustrations, text and individual words, enabling all children to be familiar with the concepts and words in the text
- **Reading the text**
- **After reading:** detailed teaching notes with ideas for activities, discussion and questioning
- **ELL engagement**: tasks designed to help children who do not have English as their first language at home
- **Assessment:** ideas on how to track and keep a record of individual learning paths.

Each title's teaching notes and photocopiable worksheets comprise a range of activities that can be completed with the texts. They can be used individually, in small groups or with the whole class. The skills addressed are:

- *Comprehension*—incorporating literal or factual, inferential or interpretive, evaluative/analysing and applied/creative comprehension within specific comprehension skill sets including: recall, sequencing, predicting, word meaning, noun/pronoun negation, tense, cloze, paraphrasing, summarising, main idea, cause/effect, comparing/contrasting, inference, locating information, fact/opinion, figurative language, author's intent and scanning
- *Phonological awareness*—initial consonant sounds, alliteration/rhyme, manipulation of sounds, segmenting words into sounds (analysis), blending, syllables, word families, contractions, compound words, suffixes/prefixes, plurals, synonyms/antonyms, tenses and generalisations (root words, doubling last consonant)
- *Vocabulary development*—incorporating high-frequency words and topic words
- *Fluency*—including phrasing
- *Text conventions*—features of text including font emphasis, grammatical features and punctuation
- *Writing activities*—focusing on different text forms and types, e.g. recount, report, diary, procedural, narrative.

How to use *Engage Literacy* in the classroom

EXAMPLE READING LESSON

Whole class (10 minutes)

Read to children and/or share *Engage Literacy Oral Language Big Books, Engage Literacy Digital Posters*, picture storybooks or serial reading. Ensure children are exposed to varied text types, e.g. information report, procedural text, transactional, description, discussion, explanation, exposition, recount, response, narrative.

Discuss one or more of the following:
- the purpose of the text (the audience the text is intended for; author's intent; children's enjoyment of text; what they learnt from the text; meaning of the text)
- the structure of the text (layout, e.g. picture storybook; text genre; labels, headings, blurbs, verse, etc.; language flow in text, e.g. rhyme, fairy tale; grammatical features, e.g. punctuation)
- visual literacy/elements of the text (illustrations, font).

Whole class—strategy development (10 minutes)

Teach a reading strategy to the class (model/demonstrate/discuss, etc.), for example:
- how to read different genres, e.g. poems (see *Engage Literacy Digital Posters*), non-fiction, procedural text
- explore text conventions through making a class big book
- word development, e.g. brainstorm words, look at the structure of words and word meanings
- implement comprehension strategies and related comprehension skills.

Small-group activities (30 to 35 minutes)

Develop fluid, skill-based activity groups based on assessing children.

Group 1 *Teaching Group*: children work with teacher on a guided reading or reciprocal teaching activity using *Engage Literacy* fiction or non-fiction titles (or a title from the *Engage Literacy Wonder Words* pack).

Guided reading: introduce the book, walk through the text discussing pictures/key words/text conventions, read text, discuss text.

Reciprocal teaching: predicting, clarifying, generating questions, summarising.

Work with children for 10 to 15 minutes. Have them complete one of the activities or worksheet tasks related to the text. Spend the remaining time in the lesson roving among the other groups, teaching and refining reading strategies that the children are using.

Groups 2 and 3 *Independent Reading Tasks*: children work independently on tasks that help develop reading strategies (e.g. read silently, summarise texts, diary/journal writing, make up new titles for stories, supply an alternative ending).

These activities can be varied to suit the needs of the children, e.g. the activities can be related to:
- a text the children have been reading, using the *Teacher's Resource* suggested tasks and worksheets as a guide
- a text the whole class has been listening to
- a 'stand-alone' reading activity that does not relate to a particular text.

Note: Oral Language Big Books provide independent vocabulary development activities related to the scene (see the inside front/back cover of the *Oral Language Big Books*).

Whole-class sharing (5 to 10 mins)

Have children share the skills and discoveries that were developed over the lesson through discussion/demonstration. Based on your observations during the lesson, teach or highlight a particular skill that would be beneficial to the children.

Assessment

Assessment needs to be ongoing and continuous in order to ascertain the changing developmental level of a child. Information that can be gathered to determine a child's level includes: anecdotal information, observations, Running Records and previously completed tasks. Once a reading level has been established, place the child at the appropriate reading level. Each level matches the *Engage Literacy* colour coding for easy reference (see page iv).

Running Records for each *Engage Literacy* text are provided in the *Teacher's Resource* (see page viii and pages 121 to 144) to help with ongoing monitoring and assessment.

How to use the Running Records

Running Record sheets for each Engage Literacy title are provided at the back of the *Teacher's Resource* books.

What is the purpose of a Running Record?

- A Running Record provides a diagnostic assessment of a child's reading ability.
- A Running Record looks at the strategies a child uses to read and is a useful tool for informing planning.
- A Running Record informs you if a book is suitable for a child's reading level.

Preparation

- Select a book that the child is familiar with.
- Explain to the child that you are going to listen to them read aloud because you are looking at their reading.
- Introduce the book to the child by looking at the front cover and the title page.
- When you are ready, ask the child to start reading.

Making a Running Record

- Using the reading symbols outlined below, mark the text on your Running Record as the child reads. Record a mark above each word. Use the first two columns on the right to keep a tally of the number of errors and self-corrections.
- Refer to the reading strategies outlined below, and note the reading strategies used in the final column.

Reading symbols

<u>No errors</u>
✓ = correct word
R = repeated word
Sc = self-corrects

<u>Errors</u>
O = omitted word
^ = inserted word (write the inserted word above the text)
T = told word (if the child attempts the word, write the attempt over the word and record it as an error unless the child manages to say the word correctly)

Reading strategies

Ph = phonic	the child tried to sound out the problem word
G = graphic	the child suggested a word that looks similar to the problem word
S = syntactic	the child suggested a grammatically sensible word
C = contextual	the child suggested a sensible substitution within the context of the whole text

Interpreting the Running Record

Count up the total number of errors (do not include self-corrections) and calculate the accuracy rate using the formula outlined below:

$$\frac{\text{Number of words read accurately}}{\text{The total number of words}} \times 100$$

So for example, if a child read 114 words correctly in a 126-word book, the accuracy rate would be:

$$\frac{114}{126} \times 100 = 90.5\%$$

A reading accuracy rate of 95% or above indicates that the book is at a comfortable level for the child to read independently. A reading accuracy rate of between 90% and 95% signifies that the text is appropriate for use during a guided reading lesson. Below 90% indicates that the text is too difficult.

Notes made during the Running Record should indicate which strategies the child is using to read. If the child is relying heavily on one strategy, he or she may need support using other strategies.

Our Baby

Level 15 **Fiction** **Word count:** 282 **Text type:** Narrative

HFW introduced: just, much, soon, when
HFW consolidated: didn't, maybe, peeped, thing
Linking texts: *Growing Up* (non-fiction); *Digital Poster 'Me'*
Curriculum link: me/family, community
Phonic awareness: digraphs 'ou', 'wh'; contractions 'didn't', 'that's', 'where's'; syllables; suffixes 'ed', 'ing'; split digraph 'o_e'; final consonant blends 'nd', 'ng', 'nt'
Story summary: Rosie is waiting and waiting for the baby to come. One morning when Rosie wakes up, Granny takes Rosie to the hospital to see her mum, dad and their new baby boy.

Tuning in

- Talk about babies. Ask, *What are babies like? Have you got a baby brother or sister? Have you seen a baby growing in a mummy's tummy before? Where does the mummy go to have her baby?* Discuss what babies look like and how they are different from other children. Have children role-play being a baby. Ask, *Can you crawl like a baby? Can you cry like a baby?*

Book walk

- Introduce the story. Give each child a copy of the book and discuss the title. Ask, *How many words are in the title? Can you see any words you know?* Have children predict words that might be in the text. Discuss the illustration on the front cover and link to children's personal experiences. Ask, *What do you think this story is going to be about? What do you think the characters are going to do?*
- Flip through the book, discussing events and illustrations. Promote language that is used throughout the text. Discuss how illustrations help us to read the text. When questioning, use vocabulary from the text.

  pages 2–3: Ask, *Who is Rosie looking at? Who has a big, round tummy? When do you think the baby will come?*
  pages 4–5: Ask, *Is Mum's tummy still big and round the next day? Do you think Rosie wants the baby to come? Did the baby come today?*
  pages 6–7: Ask, *Where has Rosie put her hand? What did she rub up and down on Mum's tummy? Where has she put her cheek? Do you think the baby would answer Rosie when she says 'hello'?*
  pages 8–9: Ask, *Who was on the couch the next morning when Rosie woke up? Where do you think Mum and Dad are? Why would Mum and Dad be at the hospital? Who is coming today?*
  pages 10–11: Ask, *What did Granny and Rosie go in to get to the hospital? What colour is the taxi? Where did the taxi take them?*
  pages 12–13: Ask, *What are Granny and Rosie walking past? Are any of these their baby? Where do you think their baby is?*
  pages 14–15: Ask, *What did Granny and Rosie see when they peeped around the door? Who do you think has missed Rosie? What is Mum sitting on? Is her tummy big and round? What did Rosie see next to Dad?*
  page 16: Ask, *Is that their baby? Why are they all smiling?*

Reading the text

- Have children read independently. Focus on meaning, structure and visual cues. Support development of reading strategies. Identify areas that challenge children and can be developed into future learning experiences.
- Discuss reading strategies with children. During reading ask, *How could you work out this word? Did that make sense?* Encourage children to go back and self-correct.
- Ask children to relate the story to their own experiences. Ask, *Has your mum had a baby? Is there a baby in your family?*
- Have children retell the story in their own words. Talk about the beginning, middle and end of the story.
- Discuss how this text is a narrative and talk about the orientation, complication and resolution of the story.
- Talk about the characters and their role in the story.
- Ask inferential questions such as: *Why is Mum's tummy big and round? Why was Rosie putting her hand and cheek on Mum's tummy? Why didn't the baby say anything? Why was Granny in the house? Why did Rosie and Granny take a taxi to the hospital? Why isn't Mum's tummy big and round any more?*

After reading

Focus on meaning, structure and visual cues that children found difficult while reading. Discuss strategies and provide opportunities for children to consolidate specific skills. For example, if children had difficulty with the word 'hospital', discuss strategies such as sounding out, re-reading or looking at the illustrations.

Choose from the following activities.

Comprehension

- *Sequencing:* Have children recall the events of the story. Ask, *What happened in the beginning/middle/end of the story?* Ask children to talk about what the characters did throughout the story. Ask, *What was Rosie doing in the beginning of the story? What was Mum doing at the end*

of the story? Write sentences from different pages of the text on strips of paper. Give each child a strip of paper and have them read the sentences and sequence them in the correct order. Have children complete **PW 1** (page 3), sequencing the sentences and pasting them in the correct order on a strip of paper. Children can add matching pictures under each box.
- *Summarising:* Turn to pages 2–3 and have children re-read the text and look at the illustrations. Ask children to summarise what happened at this part of the story. Discuss how summarising means identifying the most important things. Ask, *What was the main thing that happened at this part of the story?* Record children's responses. Repeat with the remaining pages.

Phonological awareness
- Talk about the word 'our'. Discuss the vowel digraph 'ou' and the sound these letters make when sounded together. Have children brainstorm other 'ou' words, e.g., 'out', 'house', 'hour'.
- Talk about the contractions in the text: 'didn't', 'that's' and 'where's'. Discuss how a contraction has an apostrophe to show that two words have been joined. Write 'did not' and 'didn't' and show how the apostrophe is written instead of the 'o' when the words are joined. Repeat for 'that's' and 'where's'. Find the contractions in the text. Have children complete **PW 2** (page 4), cutting out the words in boxes and matching them to the contractions.
- As a group, clap the syllables in 'hospital'. Ask, *How many syllables are in this word?* Discuss the beginning and ending sounds in the word. Count the number of syllables in other words from the text.
- As a group, find 'coming' in the text. Talk about the sound 'ing' makes at the end of the word. Brainstorm and record other 'ing' words.
- Talk about the 'ed' suffix. Have children find words in the text that end with 'ed' and practise reading them. Talk about how 'ed' on the end of a word means it has already happened (i.e. past tense).
- Discuss 'woke' and the split digraph 'o_e'. Brainstorm other 'o_e' words, e.g., 'pole', 'hope', 'home'.
- Talk about the final consonants 'nd'. Discuss how these letters are blended together to make one sound. Find 'hand' in the text and have children identify the 'nd' blend. Talk about the other final consonant blends in the text: 'ng' and 'nt'. Have children practise blending these sounds and find them in the text.
- As a group, talk about the consonant digraph 'wh' in 'when'. Talk about how these letters make one phoneme, rather than being spoken separately as 'w-h'. Model the sound these letters make together. Ask children to find other 'wh' words in the text.

Vocabulary
- *Visual recognition of high-frequency words:* 'just', 'much', 'soon', 'when'. Ask children to find these words in the text. Write the words on cards (two cards for each word) and play games such as Concentration and Snap.
- Have children make a wordsearch using the high-frequency words.

Fluency
- Discuss the importance of reading smoothly and without stopping. Demonstrate how to read fluently. Have children practise by reading pages of the text to each other.

Text conventions
- *Sentence features:* Discuss how sentences begin with an upper-case letter and end with a full stop, exclamation mark or question mark. Turn to different pages of the text and ask, *How many sentences are on this page? How do you know where the sentence starts? How do you know where the sentence ends?* Have children count the number of sentences in the text.
- *Text emphasis/bold font:* Talk about how some words in the text are bold. Discuss how we use a bigger voice or emphasise these words as we read them. Turn to page 8 and have children practise this skill by reading the sentences and changing their tone for the bold text.

Writing
- Have children recall why Rosie's mum went to hospital. Talk about why people might need to go to hospital. Discuss how doctors and nurses are at hospitals to help look after people. Have children write a text that explains why hospitals are important. Have them use sound–letter correspondence in their writing.

▶ ELL engagement
- Talk about the different people in families. Ask, *Who is in your family?* Have children brainstorm and record people who could be in a family, e.g. mum, dad, brother, sister, aunty, uncle, granny, grandpa, baby, cousin. Have children draw a picture of their family and label the people in the picture.
- Have children talk about babies and the things that they need. Ask, *What have you got at home to help look after your baby brother or sister?* Talk about things that babies don't need. Discuss how some things are dangerous for babies. Bring in a variety of baby items such as nappies, toys and dummies. Ask children to name and describe each item. Ask, *What would we use this for if we looked after a baby?* Support and enhance children's language development during discussions. Have children complete **PW 3** (page 5), sorting pictures of things babies need and don't need into columns.

▶ Assessment
- PWs 1, 2 and 3 completed
- Note the child's responses, attempts and reading behaviours before, during and after reading
- Collect work samples, e.g. PW 1 could be kept in the child's portfolio
- Complete Running Record (page 121)

Name: ______________________ Date: ____________

PW 1

Sequencing

You will need: coloured pencils, scissors, glue, long strip of paper

- Cut out the boxes and put them in the correct order.
- Paste the boxes in order on the strip of paper.
- Draw pictures to match under each box.

The next morning, when Rosie woke up,
Granny was sitting on the sofa.
"Mum and Dad are at the hospital," said Granny.

Rosie looked at Mum. Here tummy was big and round.
"When will our baby come?" asked Rosie.
"Soon," said Mum.

Granny and Rosie walked by lots of babies.
"Is this our baby?" asked Rosie.
"No," said Granny. "That's not our baby."

Granny and Rosie got into a big yellow taxi.
They went down the street and up the hill.

The next day, Rosie put her hand on Mum's tummy.
Then she put her cheek on top. "Hello, Baby," she said.
But the baby didn't say a thing.

Mum was sitting up in bed.
Her tummy was not big and round. Rosie saw a little bed.
"Is this our baby?" asked Rosie. "Yes!" smiled Mum.

Main teaching focus
Comprehension: Sequencing events from the text.

Other teaching focus
Comprehension: Visualising—drawing pictures to match sentences.

Teacher's note
Children cut out the boxes and put them in the correct order. They then paste them on a strip of paper and draw matching pictures.

Engage Literacy is published in 2013 by Raintree • *Our Baby*, Level 15. This page may be photocopied for educational use within the purchasing institution.

Name: ______________________ Date: ______________

Contractions

You will need: scissors, glue

- Cut out the boxes at the bottom of the page.
- Match and paste them under the correct contractions.

didn't	that's	where's	let's

I'm	can't	don't	it's

✂

let us	can not	did not	where is
I am	do not	that is	it is

Main teaching focus
Grammatical knowledge: Contractions.

Other teaching focus
Text conventions: Apostrophes for contractions.

Teacher's note
Children cut out the boxes at the bottom of the page, then match and paste them under the contractions.

Engage Literacy is published in 2013 by Raintree • *Our Baby*, Level 15. This page may be photocopied for educational use within the purchasing institution.

Name: ______________________ Date: ______________

What does a baby need?

You will need: coloured pencils, scissors, glue

- Colour and cut out the pictures.
- Paste the things a baby needs under the ✔.
- Paste the things a baby doesn't need under the ✘.

✔	✘

Main teaching focus
Oral language: Discussion and awareness of the needs of babies.

Other teaching focus
Oral language: Comparing and contrasting items; discussing an object's purpose.

Teacher's note
Children colour and cut out the pictures. They sort the items into two groups—*things babies need* and *things babies don't need*. Children then paste the pictures in the appropriate columns.

Engage Literacy is published in 2013 by Raintree • *Our Baby*, Level 15. This page may be photocopied for educational use within the purchasing institution.

What is the Matter, Mrs Long?

Level 15 **Fiction** **Word count:** 287 **Text type:** Narrative

HFW introduced: could, just, knock, matter, must, purple, sudden, when
HFW consolidated: as, well, what
Linking texts: *Letter to Sam* (non-fiction); *Digital Poster 'The Lady with the Crocodile Purse'*
Curriculum link: community, celebrations
Phonic awareness: digraphs 'ow', 'ou', 'ee', 'ck', 'th'; root word 'ill'; suffix 'ing'
Story summary: Mrs Long feels ill when she sees a tiger, a dinosaur and a fairy. Mr Lee takes her to the doctor and he sees them too! It turns out to be children dressed up for Halloween.

Tuning in

- Ask children to talk about a time when they have felt ill. Ask, *What is a synonym for the word 'ill'? What made you feel sick? What did you do to get better? Did you go and see the doctor when you were sick?*
- Talk to children about Halloween. Ask children if they have dressed up in costumes or if they have gone 'trick or treating'. Talk about why it is important to have a trusted adult with you if you go 'trick or treating'.

Book walk

- Introduce the story. Give each child a copy of the book and discuss the title. Ask, *How many words are in the title? Can you see any words you know?* Have children predict words that might be in the text. Discuss the illustration on the front cover and link to children's personal experiences. Ask, *What do you think is wrong with Mrs Long? How do you think she is feeling? What do you think is going to happen?* Ask children if they think this is a real or imaginative text. Ask, *How can you tell?*
- Flip through the book, discussing events and illustrations. Promote language that is used throughout the text. Discuss how illustrations help us to read the text. When questioning, use vocabulary from the text.

  pages 2–3: Ask, *Whose shop has Mrs Long run into? Why would Mr Lee be asking her what is the matter?*
  pages 4–5: Ask, *What did Mrs Long see when she was walking down the street? Where was the black and yellow tiger running? What colour was the big dinosaur? What was the big green dinosaur doing? What colour was the little fairy? What colour was her wand?*
  pages 6–7: Ask, *Who is feeling very ill? Where do you think Mr Lee is going to take Mrs Long?*
  pages 8–9: Ask, *Who has walked out the door and is going down the street? What have they seen all of a sudden? What can they see that is black and yellow running in the park? What can they see jumping up and down? What colour is the big dinosaur? What colour fairy did they see after that? What does the fairy have in her hand?*
  pages 10–11: Ask, *Who else feels ill now? Where are they running as fast as they can?*
  pages 12–13: Ask, *Who are they talking to about what they saw when they were walking down the street? What colour tiger did they see running in the park? What type of dinosaur did they see jumping up and down? What colour fairy did they see with a purple wand?*
  pages 14–15: Ask, *Who does the doctor say is very, very ill? When they hear a knock at the door, what sound would it make? Who has come into the doctors? Who has come running in this way and that? Who is jumping up and down? Who has come in with a purple wand?*
  page 16: Ask, *Why do the children shout 'Trick or treat'?*

Reading the text

- Have children read independently. Focus on meaning, structure and visual cues. Support development of reading strategies. Identify areas that challenge children and can be developed into future learning experiences.
- Discuss reading strategies with children. During reading ask, *How could you work out this word? Did that make sense?* Encourage children to go back and self-correct.
- Ask children to relate the story to their own experiences. Ask, *Have you ever seen something that has given you a fright or made you feel ill? Have you gone trick or treating?*
- Have children retell the main parts of the story.
- Discuss how this text is a narrative and talk about the orientation, complication and resolution.
- Talk about the characters and their role in the story.
- Ask inferential questions such as: *Why do you think Mrs Long ran into the shop? Why would Mrs Long think she was ill after seeing the tiger, dinosaur and fairy? Why are they going to the doctor? Why have the tiger, dinosaur and fairy come into the doctor's house? Why are the children carrying baskets?*

After reading

Focus on meaning, structure and visual cues that children found difficult while reading. Discuss strategies and provide opportunities for children to consolidate specific skills. For example, if children had difficulty with the word 'fairy', discuss strategies such as sounding out, re-reading or looking at the illustrations.

Choose from the following activities.

Comprehension

- *Recall:* Talk about the characters. Ask, *Who were the characters in the story? What did they do?* Talk about the plot. Have children summarise what happened. Flip through the text and have children use the illustrations to help their explanations. Ask, *What happened in the beginning/middle/end of the story?* Talk about the setting. Ask, *Where did the story happen?* Have children complete **PW 4** (page 8), recording the characters, setting and plot of the story.
- *Inferring characters' feelings:* Have children name the characters. Turn to pages 2–3 and encourage children to role-play the characters' actions. Ask, *How were the characters feeling at this stage of the story?* Repeat for other pages. Have children complete **PW 5** (page 9), drawing and writing how characters were feeling.

Phonological awareness

- Talk about the vowel digraph 'ow' in 'down'. Discuss and model the sound that these letters make. Have children brainstorm other 'ow' words, e.g. 'cow' and 'now'.
- Talk about the vowel digraph 'ou' in 'out'. Discuss and model the sound that these letters make. Have children brainstorm other 'ou' words, e.g. 'shout' and 'hour'. Compare the 'ou' and 'ow' digraphs and discuss how these letters can make the same sound.
- Talk about the vowel diagraph 'ee' in 'Lee'. Discuss the sound that these letters make when they are together. Have children find other 'ee' words in the text and practise reading them.
- Talk about the final consonant digraph 'ck'. Talk about how these letters are sounded together as 'ck', rather than separately as 'c-k'. Find 'black' in the text and have children identify the 'ck' at the end of the word. Ask, *What sound would these letters make?*
- As a group, find 'ill' in the text and discuss strategies for sounding this word. Talk about how we can make new words by adding letters to the front of this word. Write 'ill' on a piece of paper and have children add letters to make new words, e.g. 'hill', 'pill', 'will', 'still', 'fill', 'spill'.
- As a group, find 'jumping' in the text. Talk about the sound 'ing' makes at the end of the word. Brainstorm and record other words that end in 'ing'. Have children circle the 'ing' suffix.
- Discuss the consonant digraph 'th'. Talk about how we sound these letters together to make one sound rather than separately as 't-h'. Have children find 'th' words in the text. Discuss how 'th' can occur at the beginning, middle or end of a word.

Vocabulary

- *Visual recognition of high-frequency words:* 'could', 'just', 'knock', 'matter', 'must', 'purple', 'sudden', 'when'. Ask children to find these words in the text. Write the words on cards (two cards for each word) and play games such as Concentration and Snap.

Fluency

- Discuss the importance of reading smoothly and without stopping. Demonstrate how to read fluently. Have children practise by reading pages of the text to each other.

Text conventions

- *Question marks:* Talk about how question marks are at the end of a question rather than a full stop. Encourage children to identify the question mark on page 3. Have children ask each other questions and record them on a piece of paper with a question mark at the end.
- *Speech marks:* Discuss speech marks. Explain that text between the speech marks is what a character is saying. Have children identify speech marks in the text. Write the text from pages 6–7 on a sheet of paper. Tell children to colour over the words that are between the speech marks. Have them role-play the conversation by reading the text between the speech marks.

Writing

- Have children look at and describe the picture on pages 8–9. Ask, *What are the characters doing? How do you think they feel? Where are they? What are they going to do next?* Ask children to write a description of this picture.
- Talk about how adjectives are words that describe things. Turn to pages 4–5 and support children in finding the adjectives, e.g. 'big', 'green'. Explain how these words describe the dinosaur. As a group, think of adjectives to describe other characters in the story. Have children complete **PW 6** (page 10), writing adjectives to describe Mr Lee and Mrs Long.

▶ ELL engagement

- Provide a variety of costume items for children to wear and look at. Have children describe each other while they are wearing the costumes. Support children in using adjectives. Encourage them to role-play different people while wearing the costumes.
- Talk about doctors and what they do and what they use, e.g. thermometers, stethoscopes. Discuss how when people go to the doctor, they are called a 'patient'. Have children role-play being a doctor and a patient. Ask children to draw and label a picture of themselves going to the doctor.

▶ Assessment

- PWs 4, 5 and 6 completed
- Note the child's responses, attempts and reading behaviours before, during and after reading
- Collect work samples, e.g. PW 4 could be kept in the child's portfolio
- Complete Running Record (page 122)

Name: ____________________ Date: ____________

PW 4

What did they do?

You will need: coloured pencils

- Draw the characters and what they were doing at the different settings in the story.
- Write what the characters were doing under the pictures.

____

____

____

____

Main teaching focus
Comprehension: Recalling the characters, setting and plot of the story.

Other teaching focus
Writing: Writing sentences to match pictures.

Teacher's note
Children draw the characters at different settings in the story and what they were doing. They then write sentences under the pictures to explain their drawings.

Engage Literacy is published in 2013 by Raintree • *What is the Matter, Mrs Long?*, Level 15. This page may be photocopied for educational use within the purchasing institution.

Name: ______________________ Date: ______________

How did they feel?

You will need: coloured pencils

- Draw the characters' faces to show how they were feeling.
- Write sentences to explain why they felt like that.

____

____

____

____

Main teaching focus
Comprehension: Inferring characters' feelings.

Other teaching focus
Writing: Using upper-case letters and full stops in writing.

Teacher's note
Children draw the expressions on Mrs Long and Mr Lee's faces to show how they were feeling. They then write sentences to explain why they were feeling that way.

Engage Literacy is published in 2013 by Raintree • *What is the Matter, Mrs Long?*, Level 15. This page may be photocopied for educational use within the purchasing institution.

Name: ______________________ Date: ______________

PW 6

Adjectives

- Write adjectives to describe things in the picture, e.g. 'pretty' (hat), 'large' (feet).
- Draw lines from the adjectives to the picture.

Main teaching focus
Writing: Using adjectives.

Other teaching focus
Oral language: Identifying and naming familiar objects; describing items.

Teacher's note
Children write adjectives to describe different parts of Mrs Long and Mr Lee. They draw lines from the picture to the adjectives.

Engage Literacy is published in 2013 by Raintree • *What is the Matter, Mrs Long?*, Level 15. This page may be photocopied for educational use within the purchasing institution.

Growing Up

Level 15 **Non-fiction** **Word count:** 297 **Text type:** Report

HFW introduced: could, hold, just, lift, older, own, rest, when, would, year/s

HFW consolidated: been, five, four, herself, himself, their, things, what

Linking texts: *Our Baby* (fiction); *Digital Poster 'You Grow Up, Too'*

Curriculum link: me/family, community, physically active

Phonic awareness: segmenting CVCC words; rhyming words 'look', 'book'; digraphs 'ee', 'ay'; phonemes 'ar', 'ould'

Text summary: Every year you grow older, and you learn to do lots of new things. Find out what new things children are able to do as they grow from one year old to five years old!

Tuning in

- Have children talk about what they were like when they were babies. Ask, *What did you look like when you were little? What things can you do now that you couldn't do when you were a baby?* Make a list of children's responses.
- Show photos of children and babies. Ask, *What types of things would this child/baby be able to do?* Discuss how the older children are, the more things they are capable of.

Book walk

- Introduce the text. Give each child a copy of the book and discuss the title. Ask, *How many words are in the title? Can you see any words you know?* Have children predict words that might be in the text. Discuss the photographs on the front cover and link to children's personal experiences. Ask, *What do you think this text is going to be about? Do you think this is going to be an information or a story book?*
- Flip through the book, discussing events and pictures. Promote language that is used throughout the text. Discuss how pictures help us to read the text. When questioning, use vocabulary from the text.

pages 2–3: Ask, *What is the mum holding? How old do you think the baby is? Does everybody look like this when they are born? What could you do when you were a bit older? Where is this baby resting her tummy? What can she do with her head?*
pages 4–5: Ask, *What can this baby do? What do you think this baby says? Can you remember if you said 'Goo-ga' when you were a baby? What is this baby doing? Can this baby smile and laugh? Who is holding her bottle?*
pages 6–7: Ask, *How old is this baby? Do you think he can walk by himself? What does he like to eat? What can babies say when they are one? Can you remember if you said 'Mumma', 'Dadda' or 'bubba'?*
pages 8–9: Ask, *How old is a toddler? Do you think she can jump up and down? What can she hold in her hand? Can a toddler do new things?*
pages 10–11: Ask, *How old is this boy? Where do some children go when they are three? What can this boy make with the blocks? Do you think he can do up his own buttons? Can children talk a lot when they are three?*
pages 12–13: Ask, *Where do lots of children go when they are four? Can children paint when they are at nursery? What can this boy do when he is four? Do they like to look at books? Who do they like to play with? Did you play with your friends at nursery?*
pages 14–15: Ask, *How old is this little girl? Where do you think she has just started to go? Do you think she can skip, and get dressed by herself? Can she start to read now that she is five? What things can you do when you are older?*
page 16: Ask, *Why are these words and pictures here? How would these words help us read the text? What do these words mean?*

Reading the text

- Have children read independently. Focus on meaning, structure and visual cues. Support development of reading strategies. Identify areas that challenge children and can be developed into future learning experiences.
- Discuss reading strategies with children. During reading ask, *How could you work out this word? Did that make sense?* Encourage children to go back and self-correct.
- Ask children to relate the text to their own experiences. Ask, *What were you like when you were a baby? What things could you do when you were one/two/three/four/five?*
- Have children summarise the text in their own words.
- Discuss how this is an information text. Ask, *Why can't a baby walk? Why do babies say 'Mumma', Dadda' and 'bubba'?*

After reading

Focus on meaning, structure and visual cues that children found difficult while reading. Discuss strategies and provide opportunities for children to consolidate specific skills. For example, if children had difficulty with the word 'crawl', discuss strategies such as sounding out, re-reading or looking at the illustrations.

Choose from the following activities.

Comprehension

- *Sorting/comparing and contrasting:* On a large sheet of paper, write the ages 0–5 down the left-hand side. Ask children what the babies/children were able to do at each age. Record their responses next to the appropriate number. Have children complete **PW 7** (page 13), sorting the sentences into the appropriate columns of the chart.
- *Sequencing:* Ask children to flip through the text and talk about what the children were able to do at different ages. Write sentences from the text on strips of paper. Give the sentences to the children to sort into the correct order. Discuss strategies for completing the task, such as finding the things that babies are able to do first. Ask children to draw matching pictures.

Phonological awareness

- Find 'jump' in the text. Have children practise segmenting the word 'jump'. Repeat with the words 'h-o-l-d', 'r-e-s-t' and 'l-i-f-t'.
- Talk about rhyming words. Have children find 'look' and 'book' in the text. Discuss how these words have the same letters at the end. Explain how words that sound the same at the end are rhyming words. Ask, *Can you think of other words that rhyme with 'look' and 'book'?*
- Talk about the vowel digraph 'ee' in 'been'. Model the sound these letters make. Have children think of other 'ee' words. Record these words and have children circle the 'ee' digraph.
- Discuss the vowel digraph 'ay'. Talk about how we sound these letters together, rather than separately as 'a-y'. Have children find 'ay' words in the text.
- Talk about how the letters 'ar' make one phoneme. Find 'started' in the text and model how to read this word by sounding the 'ar' in the middle of the word. Have children think of and record other 'ar' words.
- Discuss the 'ould' phoneme in 'could'. Model the sound that these letters make. Ask children to think of words that rhyme with 'could', e.g. 'would', 'should'. Record these words and have children circle the 'ould' phoneme in each.

Vocabulary

- *Visual recognition of high-frequency words:* 'could', 'hold', 'just', 'lift', 'older', 'own', 'rest', 'when', 'would', 'year/s'. Ask children to find these words in the text. Write the words on cards (two cards for each word) and play games such as Concentration and Snap.
- Ask children to put the high-frequency words in alphabetical order.

Fluency

- Discuss the importance of reading smoothly and without stopping. Demonstrate how to read fluently. Have children practise by reading pages of the text to each other.

Text conventions

- *Sentence features:* Discuss how sentences begin with an upper-case letter and end with a full stop, exclamation mark or question mark. Turn to different pages of the text and ask, *How many sentences are on this page? How do you know where the sentence starts? How do you know where the sentence ends?* Ask children to count how many sentences there are.
- *Text emphasis/bold font:* Discuss the bold word on page 15. Discuss how we use a bigger voice or emphasise these words as we read them. Have children practise this skill by reading the text on page 15 and changing their tone for the bold text.
- *Commas:* As a group, discuss commas and have children identify the commas in the text. Talk about how we pause at a comma when we are reading. Model this to children and then have them practise, using sentences from the text. Have children complete **PW 8** (page 14), identifying the commas, upper-case letters, full stops, exclamation marks and question marks.

Writing

- Have children talk about the things they could do when they were a baby, a toddler, at nursery and at school. Ask children to predict things that they will be able to do when they are older—a teenager or an adult. Ask them to finish the sentences: 'When I am a teenager ...', 'When I am an adult ...' Ensure they write about the things they will be able to do then that they aren't able to do now. Support children in using upper-case letters and full stops in their writing.

▸ ELL engagement

- Ask children to bring in photos of when they were little and photos of themselves now. Have them look at the pictures and comment on how they are the same and how they are different. Provide photos of other people such as grandparents, teenagers, mums and dads for children to look at and discuss. Encourage children to compare and contrast their appearance and also the things that they would or wouldn't be able to do. Support and extend children's language development during discussions. Have children complete **PW 9** (page 15), comparing and contrasting the pictures of people.

▸ Assessment

- PWs 7, 8 and 9 completed
- Note the child's responses, attempts and reading behaviours before, during and after reading
- Collect work samples, e.g. PW 7 could be kept in the child's portfolio
- Complete Running Record (page 123)

Name: ______________________ Date: ______________

Sorting

You will need: scissors, glue

- Cut out the sentences.
- Paste them into the correct boxes.

This boy is three years old. He can go to nursery.	This baby can walk by himself, and he likes to eat baby food!	This little girl is five years old. She has just started school.
This girl can skip. She has just started to read.	This boy can do up his own buttons. He can talk a lot, too!	This baby can say, “Mumma”, “Dadda” and “bubba”.

Main teaching focus
Comprehension: Sorting sentences; comparing and contrasting.

Other teaching focus
Comprehension: Recalling events from the text.

Teacher's note
Children cut out the sentences and sort them into the appropriate group—one year old, three years old or five years old. They then paste them into the table.

Engage Literacy is published in 2013 by Raintree • *Growing Up*, Level 15. This page may be photocopied for educational use within the purchasing institution.

PW 8

Name: ____________________ Date: ____________

Sentences

You will need: coloured pencils

- Colour the capital letters red. (ABC)
- Colour the full stops blue. (.)
- Colour the exclamation marks yellow. (!)
- Colour the question marks green. (?)
- Colour the commas purple. (,)

Lots of children go to nursery when they are four.
Children at nursery can paint.
They can hop on one leg, too.
They love to look at books and play
with their friends.
Did you play with your friends
when you were at nursery?

This little girl is five years old.
She has just started school.
There are lots and lots of things she can do.
She can skip. She can dress herself.
She has also just started to read!
Did you start to read when you were five?
Now that you are older, what can you do?

I found ____ capital letters. (ABC)
I found ___ full stops. (.)
I found ____ exclamation marks. (!)
I found ___ question marks. (?)
I found ____ commas. (,)
I found ____ sentences.

Main teaching focus
Text conventions: Identifying upper-case letters, full stops, exclamation marks, question marks, commas and sentences.

Other teaching focus
Text conventions: Features of a sentence.

Teacher's note
Children identify and colour the punctuation marks according to the instructions. Children count and record how many there are in the passage. They then count the number of sentences.

Engage Literacy is published in 2013 by Raintree • *Growing Up*, Level 15. This page may be photocopied for educational use within the purchasing institution.

Name: ______________________ Date: ____________

Comparing and contrasting

- Look at the pictures.
- Write how these people are the same and how they are different.

How are they the same?	How are they different?

How are they the same?	How are they different?

Main teaching focus
Oral language: Comparing and contrasting.

Other teaching focus
Writing: Using upper-case letters and full stops in writing.

Teacher's note
Children compare and contrast the pictures, then record the similarities and differences in the boxes.

Engage Literacy is published in 2013 by Raintree • *Growing Up*, Level 15. This page may be photocopied for educational use within the purchasing institution.

Letter to Sam

Level 15 **Non-fiction** **Word count:** 256 **Text type:** Recount

HFW introduced: better, could, everyone, face, hope, much, purple, seven
HFW consolidated: as, brother, orange, picture/s, sick, sister, sorry
Linking texts: *What is the Matter, Mrs Long?* (fiction); *Digital Poster 'The Smile'*
Curriculum link: me/family, community, creative play, celebration
Phonic awareness: double consonants 'ss', 'tt'; phoneme 'er'; digraphs 'ow', 'wh'; split digraphs 'o_e', 'a_e'; final consonants 'ck'
Text summary: Casey writes a letter to Sam to tell him about his birthday. He had a dress-up party where they played games, ate popcorn and little cakes and had lots of fun.

Tuning in

- Talk about letters. Bring in letters for children to look at and discuss their features and purpose. Ask, *Why do people write letters? Who delivers letters? Have you ever written a letter? Have you ever received a letter?* Have children write a letter to a partner, put it in an envelope and then give it to their partner to read.
- Have children talk about birthday parties. As a group, brainstorm all the things that people do at parties.

Book walk

- Introduce the text. Give each child a copy of the book and discuss the title. Ask, *How many words are in the title? Can you see any words you know?* Have children predict words that might be in the text. Discuss the illustration on the front cover and link to children's personal experiences. Ask, *What do you think this text is going to tell us? Who do you think Sam is? What do you think the letter to Sam will be about?*
- Flip through the book, discussing events and illustrations. Promote language that is used throughout the text. Discuss how illustrations help us to read the text. When questioning, use vocabulary from the text.

pages 2–3: Ask, *Whose birthday is it? What type of party is it? Does the party look fun? Why do you think Sam wasn't at the party? Do you think people would have missed him?*
pages 4–5: Ask, *What did Akio come to the party as? Why did he look funny? What was on top of his head? What colour were his legs?*
pages 6–7: Ask, *What did Karla dress up as? What colour was her long tail? What did she have in her hair? Why do you think everyone laughed at Sally? What did Sally dress up as? What colour face and tail did she have?*
pages 8–9: Ask, *What did his sister Jill dress up as? What clown tricks do you think she showed them? What did his brother Mal dress up as? Who was helping Dad to cook the hamburgers? What did Mal put on?*
pages 10–11: Ask, *What did everyone play at the party? Who played pin-the-tail-on-the-donkey and hide-and-seek? What else did they have at the party? What came out when they hit it?*
pages 12–13: Ask, *What size cakes did they eat at the party? What else did they eat? What cake did Gran make for him? What colour was his cake? What did it look like? How many candles were on the cake? Do you think he blew out all the candles?*
pages 14–15: Ask, *Who dressed up as the tiger? What colour was his face? What colour whiskers were on his face? Do you think everyone missed Sam? Do you think Sam would like all the pictures from the party?*
page 16: Ask, *Where did we see these words in the text? What do these words mean?*

Reading the text

- Have children read independently. Focus on meaning, structure and visual cues. Support development of reading strategies. Identify areas that challenge children and can be developed into future learning experiences.
- Discuss reading strategies with children. During reading ask, *How could you work out this word? Did that make sense?* Encourage children to go back and self-correct.
- Ask children to relate the text to their own experiences. Ask, *Have you ever been to a birthday party? What have you dressed up as before? Have you ever written or received a letter?*
- Have children summarise the text in their own words.
- Discuss how this text is a recount and its purpose is to tell us of someone's experience.
- Talk about how this text is a letter written to Sam. Identify and talk about the features of letters.
- Talk about who attended the party and have children compare and contrast these characters.
- Ask inferential questions such as: *Who is the boy on the front cover? What is the name of the birthday boy? How old is Casey turning? What might they be singing when they have the cake? Why do you think Casey wrote the letter to Sam? Why would Casey have put photos with the letter?*

After reading

Focus on meaning, structure and visual cues that children found difficult while reading. Discuss strategies and provide

opportunities for children to consolidate specific skills. For example, if children had difficulty with the word 'pictures', discuss strategies such as sounding out, re-reading or looking at the illustrations.

Choose from the following activities.

Comprehension

- *Matching sentences and pictures:* Say a sentence to the children and have them find the illustration in the text that would match what you said. Have children complete **PW 10** (page 18), matching the sentences to the correct picture from the party.
- *Prediction:* Talk about what happened at the end of the text. Ask, *What do you think everybody did after they had the cake? What do you think Casey did when everybody went home?* Give each child a piece of paper and have them draw a picture of what they predict happened next. When finished, have children share their predictions with the group.

Phonological awareness

- As a group, talk about the double consonants 'ss'. Find the word 'dress' in the text and ask children to point to the 'ss'. Talk about how we only sound the 's' once. Ask children if they can think of any other words that end with 'ss'. Repeat for 'tt' in 'better'.
- Find 'sister' and discuss the vowel before 'r' ending—'er'. Talk about the phoneme that these letters make when they are together. Have children find other words in the text that end with 'er' and practise sounding them.
- Talk about the long vowel digraph 'ow' and model the sound these letters make. Discuss how we sound these letters together, rather than separately as 'o-w'. Have children find 'ow' words in the text and practise reading them.
- Discuss the word 'hope' and point out the split digraph 'o_e'. Have children practise sounding 'hope'. As a group, identify other split digraphs in the text, e.g. 'cake', 'came'.
- As a group, talk about the consonant digraph 'wh' in 'white'. Talk about how these letters make one phoneme. Model the sound these letters make together. Ask children to find other 'wh' words in the text.
- Talk about the final consonant digraph 'ck'. Talk about how these letters are sounded together as 'ck', rather than separately as 'c-k'. Have children find and record words in the text that contain 'ck' and have them circle the 'ck' blend in each word.

Vocabulary

- *Visual recognition of high-frequency words:* 'better', 'could', 'everyone', 'face', 'hope', 'much', 'purple', 'seven'. Ask children to find these words in the text. Write the words on cards (two cards for each word) and play games such as Concentration and Snap.
- *Theme words—colours:* Have children find the colour words in the text. Write these words on cards and have children place each card next to an item of that colour.

Fluency

- Discuss the importance of reading smoothly and without stopping. Demonstrate how to read fluently. Have children practise by reading pages of the text to each other.

Text conventions

- *Exclamation marks:* Talk about how exclamation marks influence the way the text is read. Have children identify exclamation marks in the text. Practise reading sentences with exclamation marks and compare this with how they would be read if there were no exclamation marks.
- *Text emphasis/italic font:* Talk about how some words in the text are shown in italics. Discuss that this is because they are words that the children might not recognise, and that they are in the glossary. Show children how we can find the meaning of the words by looking at the glossary on page 16.

Writing

- Discuss how this text is a letter from Casey to Sam. Talk about the features of letters and identify these in the text. Ask, *What is the purpose of a letter? Why did Casey write this letter to Sam?* Have children discuss a personal experience of being at a party. Ask children to describe who was there and what they did. Using the template on **PW 11** (page 19), have children write a letter to someone who wasn't at the party. Ask children to write a recount of what they did and draw a 'photo'.

▸ ELL engagement

- Have children use **PW 12** (page 20) to make puppets of the characters at the party. Ask children to colour in and cut out the pictures and tape craft sticks to the back to make the puppets. Encourage children to use the puppets to re-enact the events of the text.
- Bring in a variety of 'birthday party' items, e.g. balloons, games, party hats, lollies, cakes. Help children in identifying and describing each of the items. Encourage them to use adjectives and to talk about the purpose of each item.

▸ Assessment

- PWs 10, 11 and 12 completed
- Note the child's responses, attempts and reading behaviours before, during and after reading
- Collect work samples, e.g. PW 10 could be kept in the child's portfolio
- Complete Running Record (page 124)

Name: ______________________ Date: ____________

Matching sentences and pictures

- Draw a line to match the sentence to the picture.

Akio came to the party as a big orange pumpkin.
Karla dressed up as a mermaid. She had a long purple tail and shells in her hair.
Sally dressed up as a dinosaur. She had a green face and a long green tail.
Mal dressed up as a big yellow banana. He helped Dad to cook the hamburgers.
We also had a piñata. I hit it and lots of sweets came out!
Gran made me a big orange cake that looked like a tiger.

Main teaching focus
Comprehension: Reading sentences and matching with pictures.

Other teaching focus
Comprehension: Visualising—drawing pictures to match text.

Teacher's note
Children read the sentences and draw a line to match them to the correct picture.

Engage Literacy is published in 2013 by Raintree • *Letter to Sam*, Level 15. This page may be photocopied for educational use within the purchasing institution.

Name: ______________________ Date: ____________

Write a letter

You will need: coloured pencils

- Draw a picture of your last birthday party.
- Write a letter to a friend about your birthday party.

Dear ____________________

____

____

____

____

____

____

____

____

____

From ____________________

Main teaching focus
Writing: Transactional texts—writing a letter.

Other teaching focus
Writing: Recounting a familiar topic; using upper-case letters and full stops.

Teacher's note
Children draw a picture of their birthday party in the photo space. They then write a letter to a friend about their birthday party.

Engage Literacy is published in 2013 by Raintree • *Letter to Sam*, Level 15. This page may be photocopied for educational use within the purchasing institution.

Name: ______________________________ Date: ______________

Puppets

You will need: coloured pencils, scissors, sticky tape, craft sticks

- Colour and cut out the puppets.
- Use the sticky tape to stick the craft sticks to the back of the puppets.
- Use the puppets to role-play the story.

Main teaching focus
Oral language: Role-playing with puppets.

Other teaching focus
Comprehension: Recalling events from the text.

Teacher's note
Children colour and cut out the puppets. They then attach the craft sticks to the back of the puppets using the sticky tape. Children use the puppets to role-play the text.

Engage Literacy is published in 2013 by Raintree • *Letter to Sam*, Level 15. This page may be photocopied for educational use within the purchasing institution.

Looking for Kate

Level 16 **Fiction** **Word count:** 305 **Text type:** Narrative

HFW introduced: ate, anywhere, chased, hurry, moved, other, packed, past, poor, something, underneath, you're

HFW consolidated: before, could, ever, just, sorry, sudden, would

Linking texts: *Playtime Ball Sports* (non-fiction)

Curriculum link: me/family, school, pets/animals

Phonic awareness: contraction 'you're'; split digraphs; digraph 'ee'; syllables; compound words; suffixes 'ed', 'ing', 'ly'

Story summary: Max is very sad one morning when Kate leaves for school without playing fetch. So Max gets his ball and tries to find Kate at school to play one game of fetch!

Tuning in

- Give pairs of children a tennis ball and have them role-play a game of fetch, taking turns as the dog and the owner. Ask questions such as, *Why do you think dogs like to play fetch?*
- Hide a tennis ball in the room and give children 30 seconds to try to find it. Encourage them to look above, under and behind things. When the ball has been found, ask, *Was it hard to find? How did you find it? What things have you looked for before?*

Book walk

- Introduce the story. Give each child a copy of the book and discuss the title. Ask children to visualise what they think will happen in the story. Have them make predictions, using the title and cover illustration as prompts. Ask, *Who do you think Kate is? Who do you think is looking for Kate? Why do you think the dog has a ball in its mouth?* Link to the children's personal experiences.
- Flip through the book, discussing events and illustrations. Promote language that is used throughout the text. Discuss how illustrations help us to read the text. When questioning, use vocabulary from the text.

pages 2–3: Ask, *What game do Max and Kate play every morning before school? What does Max fetch every morning?*
pages 4–5: Ask, *Is Kate playing fetch with Max this morning? Is this morning like the other mornings? Why do you think Kate might be late for school?*
pages 6–7: Ask, *How is Kate getting ready for school quickly? What is she packing into her bag? Do you think she plays with Max or runs straight to the door?*
pages 8–9: Ask, *Did Kate play fetch with Max? How does Max look? Why couldn't Kate play fetch? How did Kate go to school?*
pages 10–11: Ask, *What colour ball has Max picked up? What has Max run through? What is Max running down as fast as he can? Who is Max chasing? Is Kate too fast?*
pages 12–13: Ask, *Where is Max? What has he gone underneath to go into the school grounds? Has he found Kate at the swings? Has he found Kate at the big tree? Can he find Kate anywhere?*
pages 14–15: Ask, *Who has Kate seen? Who does Max run over to? Do you think Kate thinks Max is a good dog or a naughty dog? Who else came in through the school gate? Who will Max have to go home with?*
page 16: Ask, *What do Max and Kate play before Mum takes Max home? Why do you think they play one game of fetch?*

Reading the text

- Have children read independently. Focus on meaning, structure and visual cues. Support development of reading strategies. Identify areas that challenge children and can be developed into future learning experiences.
- Discuss reading strategies. During reading, ask, *How could you work out this word? Did that make sense?*
- Ask students to relate the story to their own experiences. Ask, *Have you ever played fetch with a dog? What happened when you were late for school one day?*
- Have children retell the story in their own words.
- Encourage children to talk about the characters and their actions and the setting and plot.
- Ask inferential questions such as: *Why was Max chasing Kate with the ball? Why didn't Kate have time to play fetch with Max? How do you think Max felt when he found Kate? Why did Mum let Kate and Max play one game of fetch before she took Max back home?*

After reading

Focus on meaning, structure and visual cues that children found difficult while reading. Discuss strategies and provide opportunities for children to consolidate specific skills. For example, if children had difficulty with the word 'quickly', discuss strategies such as sounding out the phonemes, re-reading, looking at the illustrations or using the sentence content.

Choose from the following activities.

Comprehension

- *Inferring characters' feelings:* Discuss the characters and have children recall their actions. Write the sentence starters 'I think that Kate was feeling ...' and 'I think that

Max was feeling ...' on the board. Turn to various pages and ask children to role-play different events. After each role-play, have children infer how Kate and Max would have felt. Have children verbally complete the sentence starters. Ask them to complete **PW 13** (page 23), inferring Max's feelings.
- *Sequencing:* Have children talk about the events of the story. Ask, *What happened in the beginning/middle/end?* Give each child a piece of paper and have them draw a picture of a different event from the story. Collect the children's drawings, and then as a group, have them sequence the pictures in the same order as the text. Have children complete **PW 14** (page 24), sequencing events.

Phonological awareness
- Talk about the contraction 'you're'. Write 'you are' and 'you're' on the board and discuss how the contraction has an apostrophe instead of the letter 'a'. Have children find and discuss other contractions in the text.
- Talk about how split vowel digraphs make the first vowel a long vowel. Find the words 'late', 'woke' and 'time' in the text. Have children practise sounding out the phonemes.
- As a group, find and talk about the word 'tree'. Discuss the vowel digraph 'ee' and model the sound that these letters make when they are together. Brainstorm and record other 'ee' words and have children circle the 'ee' digraph in each word.
- Discuss how many words can contain more than one syllable. Suggest some two syllable words, e.g., 'before', 'sorry', 'hurry'. Ask the children to clap the syllables.
- Have children find 'anywhere' in the text. Cover up 'where' and have children identify the word 'any', and then cover up 'any' and have children identify the word 'where'. Discuss how a compound word has two words joined together. Brainstorm and record other compound words. Have children circle the two words within each compound word.
- Talk about the suffix 'ed' and how it can be added to the end of words. Have children find words in the text that end with 'ed' and practise reading these words. Talk about how 'ed' on the end of a word means it has already happened (i.e. past tense). Repeat for 'ing' and 'ly'. Talk about how 'ly' on the end of a word shows that the word is telling us how something is being done.

Vocabulary
- *Visual recognition of high-frequency words:* 'ate', 'anywhere', 'chased', 'hurry', 'moved', 'other', 'packed', 'past', 'poor', 'something', 'underneath', 'you're'. Ask children to find these words in the text. Write the words on cards (two cards for each word) and play games, such as Concentration and Snap.
- Have children cut letters from magazines and newspapers and paste them on paper to spell the high-frequency words.

Fluency
- Discuss the importance of reading smoothly and without stopping. Demonstrate how to read fluently. Have children practise by reading pages of the text to each other.

Text conventions
- *Speech marks:* Explain that text between speech marks is what a character is saying. Have children identify speech marks in the text. Copy the text from pages 14–15 onto a sheet of paper. Tell children to colour over the words that are between the speech marks. Have them role-play the conversation by reading the text between the speech marks.
- *Exclamation marks:* Talk about how exclamation marks influence the way the text is read. Have children identify exclamation marks in the text. Practise reading sentences with exclamation marks and compare this with how they would be read if there were no exclamation mark.

Writing
- Ask children to recall what Kate needed to do to get ready for school. Encourage children to talk about how they get ready for school. Make a list of their responses on the board. Ask them to draw pictures on paper to show what they do to get ready for school. Have children use **PW 15** (page 25) to write a simple procedural text on how to get ready.

▶ ELL engagement
- As a group, talk about the things you need to do to look after a pet dog. Ask, *What do owners need to do to look after a pet dog? What things would Kate do to look after Max?* Collect and show children a variety of pet-care items, such as a collar, lead, brush, bowl and toys. Have children name and describe each item. Ask, *What would the owners use these things for?* Ask children to brainstorm other animals that people can have for pets, such as cats, birds or fish. Encourage children to discuss how owners would need to look after these different pets. Ask, *Do you look after all pets in the same way? What things would these animals need? How is the way we look after them the same or different from how we look after a dog?* Provide each child with a piece of paper and have them draw a picture of a pet they have or would like to have. Ask them to list the things they do or would do to look after their pet.

▶ Assessment
- PWs 13, 14 and 15 completed
- Note the child's responses, attempts and reading behaviours before, during and after reading
- Collect work samples, e.g. PW 1 could be kept in the child's portfolio
- Complete Running Record (page 125)

Name: ______________________ Date: ____________

PW 13

How was Max feeling?

- Write a sentence that explains how Max was feeling at that part of the story.
- Write the sentences in the bubbles.

Main teaching focus
Comprehension: Inferring a character's feelings; drawing inferences from a sentence by reasoning.

Other teaching focus
Comprehension: Recalling events in a story.

Teacher's note
Children infer how Max was feeling at different parts of the story, referring to the text if necessary. They write a sentence that explains how he was feeling in the 'thinking bubble' on each picture.

Engage Literacy is published in 2013 by Raintree • *Looking for Kate*, Level 16. This page may be photocopied for educational use within the purchasing institution.

Name: ______________________ Date: ______________

Sequencing

You will need: coloured pencils, scissors, glue, a strip of paper

- Colour and cut out the pictures.
- Sequence the pictures and paste them in the correct order on the strip of paper.

Main teaching focus
Comprehension: Sequencing events from the text.

Other teaching focus
Comprehension: Recalling what happened in the text.

Teacher's note
Children colour and cut out the pictures, then sequence the pictures and paste them in the correct order on a strip of paper.

Engage Literacy is published in 2013 by Raintree • *Looking for Kate,* Level 16. This page may be photocopied for educational use within the purchasing institution.

Name: ______________________ Date: ______________

How to get ready for school

You will need: coloured pencils

- Write or draw the things you need to get ready for school in the box.
- Write instructions on how to get ready for school.
- Draw a picture to match each of the steps.

Things I need to get ready for school

Steps

1 ______________________

____

2 ______________________

____

3 ______________________

____

4 ______________________

____

5 ______________________

____

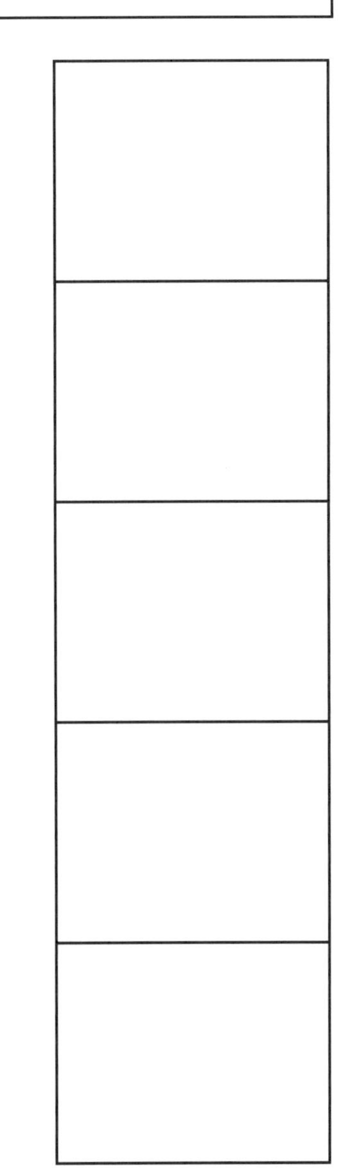

Main teaching focus	Other teaching focus	Teacher's note
Writing: Writing a simple procedural text.	*Recall:* Recalling events from the text.	Children write or draw the items they use when they get ready for school. Then they write the steps involved in getting ready for school and draw pictures to match.

Engage Literacy is published in 2013 by Raintree • *Looking for Kate,* Level 16. This page may be photocopied for educational use within the purchasing institution.

Stuck at the Top

Level 16 **Fiction** **Word count:** 339 **Text type:** Narrative

HFW introduced: beside, both, careful, enormous, forget, move, never, nice, scary, waved
HFW consolidated: could, ever, fright, gave, hold, I'll, just, much, scared
Linking text: *Wheels* (non-fiction)
Curriculum link: me/family, community, physically active
Phonic awareness: vowel digraphs 'ou', 'ow', 'ay'; rhyming words; contractions 'didn't', 'I'm', 'it's'; suffix 'ed'
Story summary: Cam and Granny are on the big wheel. Cam is having a great time, but poor Granny is scared, especially when the big wheel stops and they are stuck at the top!

Tuning in

- Talk about rides at a fair. Ask, *What rides have you been on before?* Encourage children to talk about what it feels like to go on different rides. Ask, *Have you ever been scared on a ride?*
- Have children talk about a time when they have been scared. Encourage them to show a scared expression on their face. Ask, *If you are scared of something, what things can you do?*

Book walk

- Introduce the story. Give each child a copy of the book and discuss the title. Ask children to visualise what they think will happen in the story. Have children make predictions, using the title and cover illustration as prompts. Ask, *Who do you think is stuck at the top? Where do you think they are?* Link to the children's personal experiences.
- Flip through the book, discussing events and illustrations. Promote language that is used throughout the text. Discuss how illustrations help us to read the text. When questioning, use vocabulary from the text.

pages 2–3: Ask, *What are Cam and Granny on? What is going round and round? Who is waving at Cam and Granny from down on the ground?*
pages 4–5: Ask, *Does it look like Granny is having fun or does she look scared? What can she and Cam see when they are all the way at the top? What do you think would make a big bang, crunch and screech? Where are Cam and Granny now that the big wheel has stopped?*
pages 6–7: Ask, *Does Cam look happy to be stuck at the top? Where are Cam and Granny looking? Why would Mum look like a little ant to them?*
pages 8–9: Ask, *Who is having fun when they are at the top? Why do you think Cam is swinging his seat up and down? Why do you think Granny wants Cam to stop?*
pages 10–11: Ask, *Does Granny want Cam to come and sit beside her and hold her hand or for him to stay where he is?*
pages 12–13: Ask, *Why do you think Cam is sitting as still as he can? What would make an enormous boom, brum and chug? How do you think Cam and Granny feel now that the big wheel is starting to move?*
pages 14–15: Ask, *Who helped Granny off the big wheel? Who gave Granny and Cam a big hug? Who do you think wants to go on the big wheel again?*
page 16: Ask, *Who have Mum and Cam turned around to look for? Where is Granny going?*

Reading the text

- Have children read independently. Focus on meaning, structure and visual cues. Support development of reading strategies. Identify areas that challenge children and can be developed into future learning experiences.
- Discuss reading strategies. During reading, ask, *How could you work out this word? Did that make sense?*
- Ask students to relate the story to their own experiences. Ask, *Have you ever gone on a big wheel? When have you been very scared before?*
- Have children retell the story in their own words and talk about what happened in the beginning, middle and end.
- Encourage children to talk about the characters and their actions and the setting and plot.
- Ask inferential questions such as: *Why do you think Mum did not go on the big wheel? Why did Granny walk away after she got off the big wheel? Why do you think Cam likes the big wheel? What might Granny find scary about the big wheel? Why did Mum look like a little ant? Why did Granny want Cam to sit still?*

After reading

Focus on meaning, structure and visual cues that children found difficult while reading. Discuss strategies and provide opportunities for children to consolidate specific skills. For example, if children had difficulty with the word 'ground', discuss strategies such as sounding out the phonemes, re-reading, looking at the illustrations or using the sentence content.

Choose from the following activities.

Comprehension

- *Recall:* Talk about the characters and their actions. Ask, *What did the characters do? How were they feeling?*

Discuss Cam and Granny and compare their experiences on the big wheel. Play a guessing game where children need to identify who said different phrases from the text. Turn to page 9 and read aloud: 'I'm scared and I want to come down'. Ask, *Who said that?* Turn to page 10 and read aloud: 'I'll come and sit beside you and hold your hand'. Ask, *Who said that?* Continue with other phrases. Have children complete **PW 16** (page 28), deciding which character said what.

- *Predicting:* Have children recall what happened at the end. Have children predict what would happen next time the characters saw a big wheel. Give each child a piece of paper and ask them to draw a picture of Cam, Granny and Mum next time they see a big wheel. Encourage children to write sentences to explain their predictions.

Phonological awareness

- Talk about the 'ou' digraph in the word 'round'. Talk about how these two letters make one sound rather than being sounded separately as 'o-u'. Find the 'ou' words in the text and encourage children to sound out the 'ou' digraph in these words. Repeat for 'ow'. Write the words 'round' and 'down' on the board and identify the 'ou' and the 'ow' digraphs. Discuss how these digraphs can make the same sound. Have children brainstorm and record other 'ow' and 'ou' words. Circle the digraph in each word. Have children complete **PW 17** (page 29), identifying 'ou' and 'ow' words.
- Repeat the above for the vowel digraph 'ay'.
- Have children read 'white' and 'fright' in the text. Ask, *Can you hear anything similar about these words?* Discuss how they rhyme because they sound the same at the end. Have children think of other words that rhyme with 'white' and 'fright' (e.g. 'might', 'kite'). Have children then identify 'round' and 'ground' and talk about how these also rhyme. Look at the 'ound' ending in each of these words.
- Talk about the contractions 'didn't', 'I'm' and 'it's'. Write 'did not' and 'didn't' on the board and discuss how the contraction has an apostrophe instead of the letter 'o'. Repeat for 'I'm' and 'it's'. Find contractions in the text.
- Talk about the suffix 'ed' and how it can be added to the end of words. Have children find words in the text that end with 'ed' and practise reading these words. Talk about how 'ed' on the end of a word it means it has already happened (i.e. past tense).

Vocabulary

- *Visual recognition of high-frequency words:* 'beside', 'both', 'careful', 'enormous', 'forgot', 'move', 'never', 'nice', 'scary', 'waved'. Ask children to find these words in the text. Write the words on cards (two cards for each word) and play games, such as Concentration and Snap.
- Ask children to write each of the high-frequency words in a sentence.

Fluency

- Discuss the importance of reading smoothly and without stopping. Demonstrate how to read fluently. Have children practise by reading pages of the text to each other.

Text conventions

- *Commas:* Discuss commas and have children identify the commas in the text. Talk about how readers pause at a comma when they are reading. Model this and then have children practise, using pages from the text.
- *Question marks:* Talk about how a question mark is at the end of a question rather than a full stop. Encourage children to count the question marks in the text. Have them ask each other questions and record them onto paper with a question mark at the end.

Writing

- Ask children to recall a time they have been at a fair. Have them describe what they did, what they saw and who they went with. Give children a piece of paper and ask them to draw a picture of themselves at the fair. Ask them to write a recount of their time at the fair. Support them in using upper-case letters and full stops accurately in their writing and encourage them to use a variety of time order words ('first', 'then', 'next', 'after', 'finally') to sequence and link ideas.

▶ ELL engagement

- As a group, talk about fairs. Ask, *What would you see at these events? What would you do? What would you eat?* Have children brainstorm what they would see, do and eat at a fair and record their responses. Focus on developing children's language and vocabulary. Provide children with building blocks or playdough and ask them to design and make a fair. Have each child share their model and explain the different parts. Have them make a picture of a fair by colouring and cutting out the pictures on **PW 18** (page 30) and pasting them onto a piece of paper. Ask children to draw themselves at the fair and decorate the background.

▶ Assessment

- PWs 16, 17 and 18 completed
- Note the child's responses, attempts and reading behaviours before, during and after reading
- Collect work samples, e.g. PW 16 could be kept in the child's portfolio
- Complete Running Record (page 126)

Name: ______________________ Date: ____________

Who said that?

You will need: scissors, glue

- Cut out the sentences.
- Paste the sentence under Cam if it was something that he said.
  Paste the sentence under Granny if it was something that she said.

"At last! That's one ride I will never EVER forget!"	"WOW! It's so much fun up here!"
"I'll come and sit beside you and hold your hand."	"Yippee! We are stuck right at the top!"
"Oh, no! It's a long way down."	"Please stop! I'm scared and I want to come down."

Main teaching focus
Comprehension: Recalling events from the story; matching text.

Other teaching focus
Comprehension: Inferring characters' feelings.

Teacher's note
Children cut out the sentences at the bottom of the page. They decide if each sentence was something that Cam said or something that Granny said. Children then paste the sentences in the appropriate column.

Engage Literacy is published in 2013 by Raintree • *Stuck at the Top*, Level 16. This page may be photocopied for educational use within the purchasing institution.

Name: ______________________ Date: ____________

'ou' and 'ow' words

- Add 'ou' or 'ow' to the words.
- Draw a line from the words to their matching picture.

ou		ow
__ __t		c __ __
sh __ __ t		b __ __
f __ __ nd		d __ __n
l __ __ d		cl __ __ n
h __ __ se		t __ __n
r __ __ nd		fr__ __n

Main teaching focus
Phonics: The 'ou' and 'ow' vowel digraphs.

Other teaching focus
Phonological awareness: Recognising beginning, middle and ending sounds of words.

Teacher's note
Children add the vowel digraphs 'ou' and 'ow' to the words. Then they draw a line from each word to the matching picture in the middle.

Engage Literacy is published in 2013 by Raintree • *Stuck at the Top*, Level 16. This page may be photocopied for educational use within the purchasing institution.

Name: ______________________ Date: ____________

A fair

You will need: coloured pencils, scissors, glue, a piece of paper

- Colour and cut out the pictures.
- Paste them onto a piece of paper.
- Decorate the background and draw yourself at the fair.

Main teaching focus
Oral language development: Development of language and vocabulary.

Other teaching focus
Oral language development: Relating concepts to personal experiences.

Teacher's note
Children colour and cut out the pictures. Then they paste the pictures onto a piece of paper to make a fair scene. Children can add drawings to the picture and draw themselves at the fair.

Engage Literacy is published in 2013 by Raintree • *Stuck at the Top*, Level 16. This page may be photocopied for educational use within the purchasing institution.

Playtime Ball Sports

Level 16 Non-fiction Word count: 334 Text type: Explanation

HFW introduced: anyone, anywhere, both, careful, catch, far, near, once, only, other, should, sometimes, stand

HFW consolidated: how, just, marked, must, these, when

Linking text: *Looking for Kate* (fiction)

Curriculum link: me/family, school, creative play, physically active

Phonic awareness: consonant digraphs 'ch', 'th'; vowel digraphs 'ar', 'ay', 'ee'; contractions 'don't', 'it's'; antonyms; syllables

Text summary: Find out how to play three different ball games: Down Ball, Wall Pat and Toe-touch Catchy. These games are fun to play. You can play them with your friends at school!

Tuning in

- Show children different balls and ask, *What are these balls used for? What games can you play with these balls?* Have children describe the balls and talk about how the balls are similar and different. Take the balls outside and have children demonstrate different ways of using the balls (e.g. bouncing, throwing, kicking, hitting, rolling).

Book walk

- Introduce the text. Give each child a copy of the book and discuss the title. Ask children to consider what the text will be about. Have children make predictions, using the title and cover illustration as prompts. Ask, *What ball sports do you think they are playing? When do you think they play the ball sports?* Link to children's personal experiences.
- Flip through the book, discussing events and illustrations. Promote language that is used throughout the text. Discuss how illustrations help us to read the text. When questioning, use vocabulary from the text.

pages 2–3: Ask, *What could you do with the balls at school? Where do you think these children are going to play Down Ball, Wall Pat and Toe-touch Catchy? Who do you think can play these games?*
pages 4–5: Ask, *How many squares do you need to play Down Ball? What could you use to mark the squares? Where do you and your friend need to stand?*
pages 6–7: Ask, *Where do you bounce the ball when you are ready? Where do you think your friend needs to tap the ball back to? Are the children catching the ball or tapping it? What would you need to do if you missed the ball? How could you play with four friends?*
pages 8–9: Ask, *What do you need to play Wall Pat? Is the girl standing next to the wall or a little bit away from the wall? Where does the ball go when the girl pats it with her hand? What does the ball hit once it bounces on the ground? What would you do as the ball bounces back?*
pages 10–11: Ask, *Where could you play Toe-touch Catchy at school? What do you need to play Toe-touch Catchy? How do you stand with your friend? What part of your bodies is touching? Who do you throw the ball to? Would you be good at this when you are near your friend? Would it be easy when you are further away?*
pages 12–13: Ask, *Are the boys taking a step forwards or backwards every time they catch the ball? Do you think you are allowed to drop the ball? Where do you think you must go back to if you drop the ball?*
pages 14–15: Ask, *What ball games can you see the children playing at school?*
page 16: Ask, *Where did we see these words in the text? What do these words mean?* Discuss that the glossary shows us the meaning of words that are in the text. Read the words with the children and talk about what they mean.

Reading the text

- Have children read independently. Focus on meaning, structure and visual cues. Support development of reading strategies. Identify areas that challenge children and can be developed into future learning experiences.
- Discuss reading strategies. During reading, ask, *How could you work out this word? Did that make sense?*
- Ask students to relate the text to their own experiences. Ask, *What ball games do you play?*
- Have children retell in their own words how to play the three different ball games. Encourage them to talk about how the games are the same and different.
- Discuss how the purpose of this text is to teach readers how to play the different ball games. Ask, *How would readers know how to play the games?*
- Ask inferential questions such as: *Why would these games be good to play at school? Why do the children need squares to stand in when they are playing Down Ball? Why does Toe-touch Catchy become more tricky as you step backwards?*

After reading

Focus on meaning, structure and visual cues that children found difficult while reading. Discuss strategies and provide opportunities for children to consolidate specific skills. For example, if children had difficulty with the word 'anyone', discuss strategies such as sounding out the phonemes, re-reading, looking at the illustrations or using the sentence content.

Choose from the following activities.

Comprehension

- *Comparing and contrasting:* Write the names of the three ball games on three flash cards. Have the children sit in a circle and show one of the flash cards to them. Ask the first child to recall something about the game that is shown on the flash card. Continue until all children have had a turn. Repeat with the other flash cards. When all games have been discussed, ask, *How are these games similar? What is different about these ball games?* Have children complete **PW 19** (page 33), writing how the games are the same and different.
- *Recall:* Have children recall the three ball games. Write the names of each game on a piece of paper. As a group, have children draw pictures on the paper to show how each game is played. Encourage them to write sentences explaining the rules of the game. Have children complete **PW 20** (page 34), sorting the sentences and pictures to match the correct game.

Phonological awareness

- Identify 'catchy' in the text and discuss the consonant diagraph 'ch' and how these letters are sounded as 'ch' rather than 'c-h'. Brainstorm and record 'ch' words. Repeat with 'th'.
- Find 'start' in the text. Discuss the sound made when the letters 'ar' are together. Talk about how 'start' can be read by sounding 's-t-ar-t'. Have children identify 'ar' words in the text and practise reading them. Brainstorm and record other words containing 'ar'.
- As a group, discuss the word 'play'. Talk about the vowel digraph 'ay' and model the sound these letters make together. Have children count how many times they can find 'ay' in the text. Ask children to think of other words that end with 'ay'.
- As a group, find and talk about the word 'need'. Discuss the vowel digraph 'ee' and model the sound that these letters make together. Brainstorm and record other 'ee' words. Have children circle the 'ee' digraph in each word.
- Talk about the contraction 'don't'. Write 'do not' and 'don't' on the board. Discuss how the contraction has an apostrophe instead of the letter 'o'. Repeat for 'it's'.
- Identify the antonyms 'throw' and 'catch' in the text. Discuss how antonyms are words that mean the opposite. Give children a ball and have them show how throwing and catching have opposite meanings. Find and discuss the words 'near' and 'far'. Give children a piece of paper, and as a group, have them think of and record other antonyms (e.g. 'up'/'down', 'good'/'bad'). Have children complete **PW 21** (page 35), matching the antonyms.
- Talk about syllables in words. Ask the children to listen to the following words – 'anyone', 'anywhere' – and clap the syllables.

Vocabulary

- *Visual recognition of high-frequency words:* 'anyone', 'anywhere', 'both', 'careful', 'catch', 'far', 'near', 'once', 'only', 'other', 'should', 'sometimes', 'stand'. Ask children to find these words in the text. Write the words on cards (two cards for each word) and play games, such as Concentration and Snap.
- *Action words:* As a group, talk about the word 'bounce' and how it is a verb or action word. Discuss how verbs are words that describe an action. Give children a ball so they can demonstrate the action of bouncing. As a group, find other verbs in the text.

Fluency

- Discuss the importance of reading smoothly and without stopping. Demonstrate how to read fluently. Have children practise by reading the text to each other.

Text conventions

- *Titles:* Turn to page 4 and discuss how the words 'Down Ball' are shown in large, bold font at the top of the page. Talk about how these words are similar to a title as they are telling readers what they are going to read about on these pages. Ask, *Can you find any other titles in this text?* Have children find the titles 'Wall Pat' and 'Toe-touch Catchy'. Ask, *What would readers learn about on these pages?*
- *Text emphasis/italic font:* Talk about how some words in the text are shown in italics. Discuss that this is because they are words that children might not recognise. Show children that these words are in the glossary on page 16.

Writing

- After children have had the opportunity to play the ball games in the text, ask them to retell and describe how they played the games. Have them write a recount of playing the games. Ensure they use upper-case letters and full stops accurately in their writing and encourage them to include sufficient details and information. Ask children to use a variety of time order words ('first', 'then', 'next', 'after', 'finally') to sequence and link ideas.

▸ ELL engagement

- Show children a variety of sporting equipment. Ask them to describe each item and talk about what it is used for. Focus on developing children's descriptive language and building their vocabulary. As a group, make a list of the sports and games the children know. Have children compare and contrast different sports. Encourage them to record their comparisons.

▸ Assessment

- PWs 19, 20 and 21 completed
- Note the child's responses, attempts and reading behaviours before, during and after reading
- Collect work samples, e.g. PW 19 could be kept in the child's portfolio
- Complete Running Record (page 127)

Name: ______________________________ Date: _____________

Compare and contrast

- Write how the two ball games are the same.
- Write how the two ball games are different.

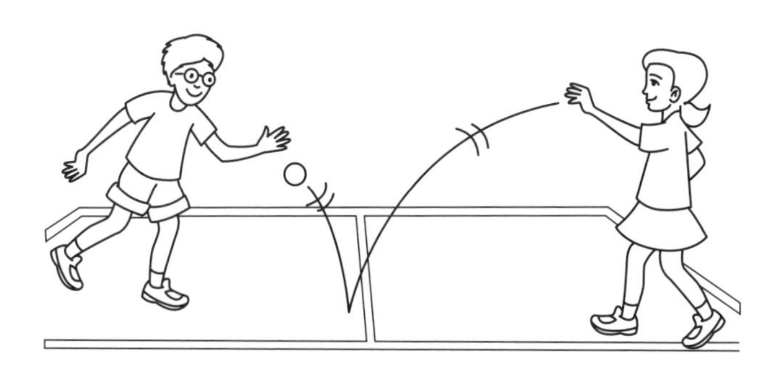

Down Ball

Toe-touch Catchy

How are the games the same?	How are the games different?

Main teaching focus
Comprehension: Comparing and contrasting information from the text.

Other teaching focus
Comprehension: Recalling information from the text.

Teacher's note
Children look at the pictures of the two ball games and recall how the games are played. Then they compare and contrast the games and write how they are the same and how they are different.

Engage Literacy is published in 2013 by Raintree • *Playtime Ball Sports*, Level 16. This page may be photocopied for educational use within the purchasing institution.

Name: ____________________ Date: ____________

Which ball game?

You will need: scissors, glue

- Cut out the sentences.
- Paste the sentences into the correct box.

Down Ball

Wall Pat

You only need a wall and a ball.

When you are ready, bounce the ball into your friend's square.

Pat the ball down with your hand once, so it bounces and then hits the wall.

Sometimes you can play with four friends and four squares.

Main teaching focus
Comprehension: Comparing and contrasting information from the text.

Other teaching focus
Comprehension: Recalling information from the text.

Teacher's note
Children cut out and read the sentences at the bottom of the page. Then they sort and paste them into the appropriate boxes.

Engage Literacy is published in 2013 by Raintree • *Playtime Ball Sports*, Level 16. This page may be photocopied for educational use within the purchasing institution.

Name: ______________________________ Date: ______________

Antonyms

You will need: coloured pencils, scissors, glue, a piece of paper

- Colour and cut out the pictures.
- Match the antonyms and paste them next to each other on the piece of paper.
- Write the words under the antonyms.

Main teaching focus
Vocabulary: Word meanings; antonyms.

Other teaching focus
Writing: Spelling—sounding out unknown words.

Teacher's note
Children colour and cut out the pictures. Then they match the pictures and paste them next to each other on a piece of paper. Children then write the words under the pictures. Encourage children to sound out unknown words.

Engage Literacy is published in 2013 by Raintree • *Playtime Ball Sports*, Level 16. This page may be photocopied for educational use within the purchasing institution.

Wheels

Level 16 **Non-fiction** **Word count:** 306 **Text type:** Report

HFW introduced: enormous, even, everywhere, heavy, move, often, roll
HFW consolidated: could, pull, small, these, think, when, would
Linking text: *Stuck at the Top* (fiction)
Curriculum link: science (transport), creative play, physically active
Phonic awareness: digraphs 'ee', 'ou', 'oy', 'wh'; syllables; compound words; split digraphs 'a_e', 'i_e'; suffix 's'
Text summary: Find out about wheels, what they do, how they help us and how you can find them everywhere. Imagine what it would be like if there were no wheels!

Tuning in

- Show children different items or pictures of things with wheels (e.g. toy cars, trolleys, skateboards, bikes). Have children identify and count all of the wheels. Ask, *Why do these things have wheels? How do the wheels help these things move?* Give each child a piece of paper and ask them to brainstorm and draw pictures of things that have wheels.

Book walk

- Introduce the text. Give each child a copy of the book and discuss the title. Ask children to consider what the text will be about. Have children make predictions, using the title and cover pictures as prompts. Have children identify all the wheels on the front cover. Link to the children's personal experiences.
- Flip through the book, discussing events and pictures. Promote language that is used throughout the text. Discuss how pictures help us to read the text. When questioning, use vocabulary from the text.

pages 2–3: Ask, *Where are the wheels on this page? What shape are wheels? How do wheels help things move? What helps move things from one place to another?*
pages 4–5: Ask, *How do you make a wheel move? Which children are pushing or pulling the wagon to move it along? What do wheels do when they move? What is going round and round on the bike?*
pages 6–7: Ask, *How do wheels help us? Could you push a heavy box along the ground? Could you push a heavy box if it was in a wheelbarrow or on a skateboard?*
pages 8–9: Ask, *What can you think of that has wheels? What do they need wheels for? Could you ride a scooter or a skateboard if they did not have wheels? Could you push a baby in a pram if it didn't have wheels?*
pages 10–11: Ask, *Where else can you find wheels? Where are the wheels at the fairground? Is a big wheel a small wheel or an enormous wheel? What is a large wheel that you find at the playground? How do the children make the roundabout spin round and round?*
pages 12–13: Ask, *What size are wheels? Can they be big and small? Are there any wheels that we can't see? Where are the wheels inside the car engine? What would the wheels inside the engine do? Where are the tiny wheels inside the watch? How do you think the tiny wheels inside the watch help it to go?*
pages 14–15: Ask, *Where do we find wheels? How do wheels help us push or pull things? How do wheels help make things work? How do wheels help us to have fun? Where can you see wheels? What would it be like if there were no wheels?*
page 16: Ask, *Where did we see these words in the text? What do these words mean?* Discuss that the glossary shows us the meaning of words that are in the text. Read the words with the children and talk about what they mean.

Reading the text

- Have children read independently. Focus on meaning, structure and visual cues. Support development of reading strategies. Identify areas that challenge children and can be developed into future learning experiences.
- Discuss reading strategies. During reading, ask, *How could you work out this word? Did that make sense?*
- Ask students to relate the text to their own experiences. Ask, *What toys do you have that have wheels? How many wheels does your car have?*
- Have children retell in their own words what wheels do, where you can find them and how they help us.
- Discuss how this is an information text that teaches readers about wheels. Ask, *What did you find out about wheels when you read this text?*
- Ask inferential questions such as: *What would happen if wheels were square instead of round? Is there a way we could move things from one place to another if there were no wheels? How are the wheels on the bike getting pushed along? Why does an aeroplane need wheels if it flies?*

After reading

Focus on meaning, structure and visual cues that children found difficult while reading. Discuss strategies and provide opportunities for children to consolidate specific skills. For example, if children had difficulty with the word 'enormous', discuss strategies such as sounding out the phonemes, re-reading, looking at the pictures or using the sentence content.

Choose from the following activities.

Comprehension

- *Cloze:* Have children recall things that they learnt about wheels while reading the text. Flip through the text and ask, *What facts did we learn about wheels on this page?* Copy sentences from the text onto paper, but leave out a word in each sentence. As a group, discuss strategies for working out the missing word. Talk about gaining meaning from the sentence and thinking about what word would make sense. Fill in the missing word. Have children re-read the sentence to check the meaning.
- *Summarising:* At the top of three pieces of paper, write the headings (one per page): 'What is a wheel?', 'Wheels help us' and 'Where we find wheels'. As a group, have children recall what they learnt about wheels and record sentences under the headings. Encourage children to draw pictures that relate to the headings. Have children complete **PW 22** (page 38), recording facts about wheels.

Phonological awareness

- Talk about the word 'wheel'. Discuss the vowel digraph 'ee' and model the sound that these letters make together. Brainstorm and record other 'ee' words and have children circle the 'ee' digraph in each word. Repeat for 'ou' ('round') and 'oy' ('toy') words.
- As a group, identify the initial consonant digraph 'wh' at the beginning of 'wheels'. Discuss how these letters are sounded to make one sound. Have children brainstorm other 'wh' words.
- As a group, clap the syllables in 'wheelbarrow'. Ask, *How many syllables are in this word?* Discuss the beginning, middle and ending sounds in the word. Count the number of syllables in other words from the text. Ask, *Can you find words in the text that have one/two/three syllables?* Have children complete **PW 23** (page 39), identifying the number of syllables in words.
- Find 'skateboard' in the text. Ask, *Can you find the two words in this word?* Cover up 'board' so that the children can see 'skate'. Then cover 'skate' so that children can see 'board'. Discuss how compound words are made of two words that are joined together. Have children find and record other compound words in the text. Ask them to circle the two words in each compound word.
- Talk about split vowel digraphs making the first vowel a long vowel phoneme. Find the words 'make' and 'ride' in the text. Have children practise sounding out these words. Ask them to find other words in the text that contain a split digraph.
- Talk about how the suffix 's' changes the way we read a word. Have children find 'wheels' in the text. Have them cover the 's' and identify 'wheel'. Discuss how the 's' on the end of the word means there is more than one wheel. Find other words with the 's' suffix in the text.

Vocabulary

- *Visual recognition of high-frequency words:* 'enormous', 'even', 'everywhere', 'heavy', 'move', 'often', 'roll'. Ask children to find these words in the text. Write the words on cards (two cards for each word) and play games, such as Concentration and Snap.
- Have children write the high-frequency words as rainbow words. Have them write the words in one colour, then in two more colours on top of the words they have already written.

Fluency

- Discuss the importance of reading smoothly and without stopping. Demonstrate how to read fluently. Have children practise by reading the text to each other.

Text conventions

- *Commas:* As a group, discuss commas and have children identify the commas in the text. Talk about how readers pause at a comma when they are reading. Model this, then have children practise using pages from the text.
- *Titles:* Turn to page 2 and discuss how the words 'What Is a Wheel?' are shown in large, bold font. Talk about how these words are similar to a title as they are telling readers what they are going to read about on these pages. Ask, *Can you find any other titles in this text? What would readers learn about on these pages?*

Writing

- Give children a building construction set that contains wheels. Have children design and build cars that have wheels. Encourage children look at how their car moves. Ask them to write a text that explains how they made their car with wheels. Ensure children include in their explanation the materials they used to make their car and the steps they took to make it.

▶ ELL engagement

- Write the words '1 wheel', '2 wheels', '3 wheels', '4 wheels' and '5 or more wheels' across the board. Discuss how things can have a different number of wheels. Have children brainstorm and record different modes of transport or objects under the appropriate words.
- Show children a picture of a big wheel. Ask, *Who has been on a big wheel?* Have children discuss what a big wheel is, where they can be found, what they do and what it feels like to go on a big wheel. Have children make their own big wheel by using the template on **PW 24** (page 40). Have children retell how they made their big wheel.

▶ Assessment

- PWs 22, 23 and 24 completed
- Note the child's responses, attempts and reading behaviours before, during and after reading
- Collect work samples, e.g. PW 22 could be kept in the child's portfolio
- Complete Running Record (page 128)

Name: ______________________ Date: ______________

Facts about wheels

You will need: coloured pencils

- Write the most important facts about wheels in the boxes.
- Draw pictures in the boxes to match your writing.

A wheel is a ...
Wheels help us to ...
We find wheels ...

Main teaching focus	**Other teaching focus**	**Teacher's note**
Comprehension: Summarising.	*Comprehension:* Recalling information from the text.	Children recall and summarise the main facts about wheels and record them in the appropriate boxes. Then they draw pictures to match their writing.

Engage Literacy is published in 2013 by Raintree • *Wheels*, Level 16. This page may be photocopied for educational use within the purchasing institution.

Name: ______________________ Date: ____________

PW 23

Syllables

You will need: scissors, glue

- Cut out the words in the boxes.
- Count how many syllables they have and paste them in the appropriate boxes.

1 syllable	2 syllables	3 syllables

wheelbarrow	skateboard	wheels
scooter	pram	tractor
train	bus	aeroplane
fairground	bicycle	roundabout
playground	push	pull
car	round	

Main teaching focus
Phonemic awareness: Syllables.

Other teaching focus
Phonemic awareness: Recognising beginning, middle and ending sounds in words.

Teacher's note
Children cut out the words and count the number of syllables. Then they paste them into the appropriate column in the table.

Engage Literacy is published in 2013 by Raintree • *Wheels*, Level 16. This page may be photocopied for educational use within the purchasing institution.

Name: ______________________ Date: ____________

Make a big wheel

You will need: coloured pencils, scissors, a split pin, glue

- Colour the parts of the big wheel and cut them out.
- Place the round wheel on top of the triangle frame.
- Put a split pin through the middle and make the wheel spin.
- Paste the seats on the big wheel.

Main teaching focus
Oral language: Language and vocabulary development.

Other teaching focus
Oral language: Retelling an experience.

Teacher's note
Children colour and cut out the pieces. Then they place the wheel on top of the triangular piece and attach with a split pin, then paste on the seats. Children may need help with this. Have children retell how they made the ferris wheel.

Engage Literacy is published in 2013 by Raintree • *Wheels*, Level 16. This page may be photocopied for educational use within the purchasing institution.

Wibbly Wobbly Tooth

Level 17 **Fiction** **Word count:** 362 **Text type:** Narrative

HFW introduced: great, happily, pulled, pushed, pushing, tried, waiting, wanted, yourself

HFW consolidated: couldn't, felt, hurt, myself

Linking text: *All About Teeth* (non-fiction)

Curriculum link: me/family, community

Phonic awareness: long vowel 'y' making 'ee' phoneme; vowel digraph 'oo'; contractions 'can't', 'couldn't'; suffix 'ed'; phoneme manipulation 'wibbly'/'wobbly'

Story summary: Luca has a wibbly wobbly tooth and everyone wants to pull it out. But Luca wants to pull it out all by himself when it is ready!

Tuning in

- Provide mirrors so children can look at their teeth. Ask, *What colour are your teeth? What do they look like? Has anybody had a wibbly wobbly tooth? Have any of your teeth fallen out?* Discuss why teeth fall out and how new teeth grow in their place.

Book walk

- Introduce the story. Give each child a copy of the book and discuss the title. Ask children to visualise what they think will happen in the text. Have children make predictions, using the title and cover illustration as prompts. Ask, *Who do you think has a wibbly wobbly tooth? What do you think will happen to his tooth? How do you think he is feeling?* Link to the children's personal experiences.
- Flip through the book, discussing events and illustrations. Promote language that is used throughout the text. Discuss how illustrations help us to read the text. When questioning, use vocabulary from the text.

pages 2–3: Ask, *Who has a wibbly wobbly tooth? How is Luca making his tooth go this way and that? Do you think Luca can push his tooth all around and make it go in and out? Is he able to pull it out?*
pages 4–5: Ask, *What do you think Dad wants to do to help Luca? Does Luca want Dad to help him or does he want to pull his tooth out when it's ready and by himself?*
pages 6–7: Ask, *What is Luca pushing? Is he pushing his wibbly wobbly tooth this way and that, and in and out? How do you think his wibbly wobbly tooth feels? Do you think his tooth hurts?*
pages 8–9: Ask, *What do you think Grandma tells Luca that he needs to pull out today? Does Luca think his tooth is ready to come out? What do you think Grandma wants to do to help Luca? Who helped Luca's father pull his tooth out when he was a little boy? Does Luca want Grandma to help him or does he want to pull his tooth out when it's ready and by himself?*
pages 10–11: Ask, *What does Luca keep pushing and pulling? Is his wibbly wobbly tooth ready to come out? Who wants to help him? What do Mum, his teacher and his best friend want to do? How do you think Luca wants to pull out his tooth?*
pages 12–13: Ask, *What is Luca doing with his wibbly wobbly tooth? How is he pushing it? Is it going in and out? What is he pushing and pulling all around?*
pages 14–15: Ask, *What has come out? Where is his wibbly wobbly tooth now? What has Luca got in his mouth now? What do you think he is happily shouting to everyone?*
page 16: Ask, *Who pulled out Luca's tooth? Did Luca pull out his tooth when it was ready?*

Reading the text

- Have children read independently. Focus on meaning, structure and visual cues. Support development of reading strategies. Identify areas that challenge children and can be developed into future learning experiences.
- Discuss reading strategies. During reading ask, *How could you work out this word? Did that make sense?*
- Ask children to relate the story to their own experiences. Ask, *Have you had a wibbly wobbly tooth? Did you pull out your tooth? Did anyone want to help you pull out your wibbly wobbly tooth?*
- Have children retell the story in their own words.
- Ask children to recall what happened in the beginning, middle and end of the story.
- Discuss the characters and their feelings at different stages of the story.
- Discuss how this text is a narrative, and talk about features of narrative text.
- Ask inferential questions such as: *Why did Luca have a wibbly wobbly tooth? Why couldn't he pull his tooth out straightaway? Why do you think everybody wanted to help Luca pull his tooth out? Why might Luca want to pull out his tooth by himself?*

After reading

Focus on meaning, structure and visual cues that children found difficult while reading. Discuss strategies and provide opportunities for children to consolidate specific skills. For example, if children had difficulty with the word 'wanted', discuss strategies such as sounding out the phonemes,

re-reading, looking at the illustrations or using the sentence content.

Choose from the following activities.

Comprehension

- *Sequencing:* Have children discuss the events. Ask, *What happened in the beginning/middle/end?* On the board, draw a table with three columns headed 'Beginning', 'Middle' and 'End'. As a group, recall events from the text and record in the appropriate columns. Flip through the text to prompt recall if necessary. Have children complete **PW 25** (page 43), sorting events from the text into beginning, middle and end categories.
- *Characters:* Have children recall the characters. Ask, *What did these characters do during the story?* Write each character's name on the top of a piece of paper and have children record each character's actions under their name. Ask, *How did these characters feel during the story?* Encourage children to record the character's feelings on the paper. Have children compare and contrast the actions and feelings of the characters.

Phonological awareness

- Find 'wibbly' in the text. Discuss how the 'y' ending makes the long vowel 'ee' sound. Have children find other words in the text with a 'y' ending that makes this sound (e.g. 'wobbly', 'ready', 'very'). Ask them to practise sounding out and reading these words.
- Discuss the 'oo' vowel digraph in 'tooth'. Explain how 'oo' in this word makes a long sound and compare it to the 'oo' in 'look', which makes a short sound. Ask children to think of other words where 'oo' makes a long sound.
- Talk about the contractions in the text: 'can't' and 'couldn't'. Write 'can not' and 'can't' on the board and discuss how the contraction has an apostrophe instead of the letters 'no'. Repeat for 'couldn't'. Find the contractions in the text.
- Talk about how the suffix 'ed' can be added to the end of words. Have children find words in the text that end with 'ed' and practise reading these words. Talk about how 'ed' on the end of a word means it has already happened (i.e. past tense).
- Identify 'wibbly' and 'wobbly' in the text. Write these words on the board and ask, *How are these words the same?* Have children identify the phoneme manipulation between the two words with the 'i' and 'o'. Discuss how a new word was made by changing one of the letters.

Vocabulary

- *Visual recognition of high-frequency words:* 'great', 'happily', 'pulled', 'pushed', 'pushing', 'tried', 'waiting', 'wanted', 'yourself'. Ask children to find these words in the text. Write the words on cards (two cards for each word) and play games, such as Concentration and Snap.
- Have children cut out letters from magazines or newspapers to make the high-frequency words and paste them onto paper.
- *Adjectives:* Discuss how the words 'wibbly wobbly' describe Luca's tooth. Look at a picture of Luca in the text and support children in thinking of adjectives to describe other parts of Luca. Ask, *How could we describe Luca's hair? How could we describe Luca's T-shirt?* Record the adjectives on the board.

Fluency

- Discuss the importance of reading smoothly and without stopping. Demonstrate how to read fluently. Have children practise by reading the text to each other.

Text conventions

- *Sentence features:* Discuss how sentences begin with an upper-case letter and end with a full stop, exclamation mark or question mark. Turn to different pages of the text and ask, *How many sentences are on this page? How do you know where the sentence starts/ends?* Discuss other sentence features such as commas and speech marks. Have children complete **PW 26** (page 44), identifying text conventions in a passage of text.

Writing

- Ask, *When did you lose your first tooth? What happened? How did you feel?* Compare the experiences of the children with Luca's experience. As a group, write a diary entry from Luca's perspective about his wibbly wobbly tooth. Start the diary entry with 'Dear Diary' and include details of what happened and how Luca was feeling. Have children complete **PW 27** (page 45), writing a diary entry about their own wobbly tooth.

▸ ELL engagement

- Have each child bring in their toothbrush and provide toothpaste, dental floss and water. Discuss the importance of brushing and looking after your teeth. Ask, *When are you meant to brush your teeth? Why do we need to brush our teeth? What do we use dental floss for?* Talk about how you need to clean the top, front and back of your teeth. Have each child brush their teeth using their toothbrush. Have children record how they brushed their teeth by writing simple sentences or drawing pictures. As a group, brainstorm vocabulary related to teeth and focus on developing and building language skills.

▸ Assessment

- PWs 25, 26 and 27 completed
- Note the child's responses, attempts and reading behaviours before, during and after reading
- Collect work samples, e.g. PW 25 could be kept in the child's portfolio
- Complete Running Record (page 129)

Name: ______________________ Date: ______________

PW 25

Beginning, middle and end

You will need: scissors, glue, a large piece of paper, coloured pencils

- Cut out the headings and groups of sentences.
- On a large piece of paper, paste the Beginning, Middle and End headings.
- Now sort and paste the groups of sentences under these headings.
- Draw pictures to show what happened in the beginning, middle and end.

Beginning	**Middle**	**End**

"I'll help you to pull it out," said Grandma.
"I pulled out your father's tooth when he was a little boy."
"No, thanks," said Luca. "I'll pull my tooth out when it's ready.
And I'll pull it out by myself!"

So Luca tried again. He pushed his tooth in and out.
The tooth went this way and that. It went in and out.
Luca pushed and pulled it all around.

Luca had a wibbly wobbly tooth.
He could push it all around but he couldn't pull it out.

Everyone wanted to help Luca pull out his tooth.
His mum wanted to help. His teacher wanted to help.
And his best friend wanted to help, too.

"Oh!" cried Luca. "My tooth came out!"
And there in his hand was his wibbly wobbly tooth.
"And," he said, "I pulled it out all by myself – when it was ready!"

"I'll pull it out for you," said Dad happily.
"No thanks, Dad," said Luca. "I'll pull my tooth out when it's ready.
And I'll pull it out by myself!"

Main teaching focus
Comprehension: Ordering events (beginning, middle, end).

Other teaching focus
Comprehension: Recalling events from the text.

Teacher's note
Children cut out the headings and sentences. On another piece of paper, they sort and paste the sentences under the Beginning, Middle and End headings. Children can draw matching pictures.

Engage Literacy is published in 2013 by Raintree • *Wibbly Wobbly Tooth*, Level 17. This page may be photocopied for educational use within the purchasing institution.

Name: ______________________ Date: ____________

PW 26

Sentences

You will need: coloured pencils

- Colour the capital letters red. (ABC)
- Colour the exclamation marks yellow. (!)
- Colour the speech marks brown. (“ ”)
- Complete the sentences at the bottom of the page.
- Colour the full stops blue. (.)
- Colour the commas purple. (,)

Luca had a wibbly wobbly tooth.

It went this way and that.

It went in and out. Luca could push it all around but he couldn’t pull it out.

“Let me take a look,” said Dad happily.

“I’ll pull your tooth out for you.”

“No thanks, Dad,” said Luca.

“I’ll pull my tooth out when it’s ready.

And I’ll pull it out by myself!”

So Luca went on pushing his wibbly wobbly tooth. He pushed it this way and that, and in and out. The wibbly wobbly tooth felt very wibbly and very wobbly. But it didn’t hurt at all!

I found ____ capital letters (ABC).

I found ____ exclamation marks (!).

I found ____ sets of speech marks (“ ”).

I found ____ full stops (.).

I found ____ commas (,).

I found ____ sentences.

Main teaching focus
Text conventions: Identifying upper-case letters, full stops, exclamation marks, commas and speech marks.

Other teaching focus
Text conventions: Features of a sentence.

Teacher’s note
Children identify and colour the sentence features according to the instructions. Children count and record the features, then count and record the number of sentences.

Engage Literacy is published in 2013 by Raintree • *Wibbly Wobbly Tooth*, Level 17. This page may be photocopied for educational use within the purchasing institution.

Name: ______________________ Date: ____________

Dear Diary

You will need: coloured pencils

- Write a diary entry about your first wibbly wobbly tooth.
- Draw a picture of you and your wibbly wobbly tooth.

Dear Diary, *Date:*

Main teaching focus
Writing: Writing a recount of a personal experience; sequencing ideas when writing.

Other teaching focus
Writing: Using upper-case letters and full stops in writing.

Teacher's note
Children write a recount (diary entry) of when they had their first wibbly wobbly tooth. Then they draw a picture of themselves with their tooth.

Engage Literacy is published in 2013 by Raintree • *Wibbly Wobbly Tooth*, Level 17. This page may be photocopied for educational use within the purchasing institution.

Lea Wants a Rabbit

Level 17 **Fiction** **Word count:** 399 **Text type:** Narrative

HFW introduced: clean, later, nowhere, owner, talk, towards, tried, wanted, yourself
HFW consolidated: about, afternoon, fresh, only, peeked, peeking, we'll
Linking text: *Animals with Fins, Animals with Fur* (non-fiction)
Curriculum link: me/family, pets/animals, community
Phonic awareness: vowel digraphs 'ea', 'aw', 'er'; contractions 'can't', 'we'll', 'I'll', 'there's'; 'y' making long vowel 'ee' sound; syllables
Story summary: Lea wants a rabbit, but Dad says he needs to think about it. After Lea explains to Dad why she would make a good pet owner, the Secret Bunny Fairy brings Lea a surprise.

Tuning in

- Ask children to think of a time when they have wanted something. Ask, *Have you asked your mum or dad for something before? What is something special that you really wanted to have?* Discuss how there are some things that we can have, some things we can't have and some things we need to wait for.

Book walk

- Introduce the story. Give each child a copy of the book and discuss the title. Ask children to visualise what they think will happen in the text. Have children make predictions, using the title and cover illustration as prompts. Ask, *Who do you think the girl on the cover is? What is she thinking about? Why do you think Lea wants a rabbit? Do you think Lea will get a rabbit?* Link to the children's personal experiences.
- Flip through the book, discussing events and illustrations. Promote language that is used throughout the text. Discuss how illustrations help us to read the text. When questioning, use vocabulary from the text.

pages 2–3: Ask, *What do you think Lea is asking Dad for? Do you think Dad said yes or no?*
pages 4–5: Ask, *Why do you think Lea says she will take good care of a rabbit? What is Lea thinking of? Why would Dad need to make a little hutch for the rabbit? Would it take a long time to make a little hutch for a little rabbit?*
pages 6–7: Ask, *What is Dad thinking about? Do you think Lea would take care of the rabbit all by herself and feed it every day? What else would Lea need to do to care for a rabbit? Do you think she and Dad will talk about it again after they go to school and work?*
pages 8–9: Ask, *What has Lea got? How is she letting her dad know that she would make a good pet owner? What is this letter for? Who wrote the letter? Who is the letter for?*
pages 10–11: Ask, *What is Dad doing? Has he made a decision or is he still thinking about it? Where are Dad and Lea? Who can Lea see getting into a little van? What did Dad open? What is on the doorstep? What is inside the small cage?*
pages 12–13: Ask, *What does Lea see when she peeks around Dad's legs? What size is the rabbit? What are the rabbit's ears like? Who is the rabbit for? What did Dad find as he opened the cage?*
pages 14–15: Ask, *What did Dad read as Lea picked up the rabbit? What is Lea giving the rabbit? What is this letter for? Who is the letter for? Who wrote the letter?*
page 16: Ask, *Do you think Lea loves her rabbit? Do you think she loves her dad? What is Dad making?*

Reading the text

- Have children read independently. Focus on meaning, structure and visual cues. Support development of reading strategies. Identify areas that challenge children and can be developed into future learning experiences.
- Discuss reading strategies. During reading, ask, *How could you work out this word? Did that make sense?*
- Ask children to relate the story to their own experiences. Ask, *Have you ever wanted a pet before? What did your mum or dad say?*
- Have children retell the story in their own words.
- Ask children to recall what happened in the beginning, middle and end of the story.
- Discuss the characters and their feelings at different stages of the story.
- Discuss how this text is a narrative and talk about the features of narrative text.
- Ask inferential questions such as: *Why do you think Lea wanted a pet rabbit? Why did Dad think about Lea having a pet rabbit before he said yes? Who might have knocked on the door? Do you think Lea would be a good pet owner? Why/why not?*

After reading

Focus on meaning, structure and visual cues that children found difficult while reading. Discuss strategies and provide opportunities for children to consolidate specific skills. For example, if children had difficulty with the word 'cage', discuss strategies such as sounding out the phonemes, re-reading, looking at the illustrations or using the sentence content.

Choose from the following activities.

Comprehension

- *Recall—characters, setting, plot:* Explain that the characters are the people in the story. Ask, *Who were the characters? What did they do?* Explain that the plot is what happened in the story. Have children summarise the plot. Flip through the text so children can use the illustrations to help their explanations. Ask, *What happened in the beginning/middle/end?* Explain that the setting is where the story took place. Ask, *Where did the story happen?* Have children complete **PW 28** (page 48), recording the characters, setting and plot.
- *Prediction:* Turn to page 16 and ask children to recall what happened at the end. Ask, *What do you think will happen next in the story?* Have children predict what Lea will do with her rabbit. Give each child a piece of paper and ask them to draw a picture of their prediction. Encourage them to share their ideas and ask, *Why do you think that will happen next?*

Phonological awareness

- Find 'clean' in the text and talk about the vowel digraph 'ea'. Model the sound that these letters make together. Have children identify other 'ea' words in the text. Ask children to record these words and circle the 'ea' in the words. Repeat for 'aw' in 'straw' and have children practise the sound.
- Talk about the contractions in the text: 'can't', 'we'll', 'I'll' and 'there's'. Write 'cannot' and 'can't' on the board and discuss how the contraction has an apostrophe instead of the letters 'no'. Repeat for 'we'll', 'I'll' and 'there's'. Have children find the contractions in the text. Ask children to complete **PW 29** (page 49), matching words to their contractions.
- Find 'owner' in the text. Discuss the sound made when the letters 'er' are together. Talk about how 'owner' can be read by sounding 'own-er'. Have children identify words containing 'er' in the text and practise reading them. Brainstorm and record other 'er' words.
- Find 'lady' in the text. Discuss how the 'y' ending makes the long vowel 'ee' sound. Have children find other words in the text with a 'y' ending that makes this sound (e.g. 'tiny'). Ask them to practise sounding out and reading these words.
- Talk about the syllables in words. Ask the children to listen to the following words and to clap for each syllable: 'nowhere', 'yourself'.

Vocabulary

- *Visual recognition of high-frequency words:* 'clean', 'later', 'nowhere', 'owner', 'talk', 'towards', 'tried', 'wanted', 'yourself'. Ask children to find these words in the text. Write the words on cards (two cards for each word) and play games, such as Concentration and Snap.
- Have children write each of the high-frequency words in a sentence.

Fluency

- Discuss the importance of reading smoothly and without stopping. Demonstrate how to read fluently. Have children practise by reading the text to each other.

Text conventions

- *Commas:* As a group, discuss commas and have children identify the commas in the text. Talk about how readers pause at a comma when they are reading. Model this and have children practise this skill using the text.
- *Speech marks:* Explain that text between speech marks is what a character is saying. Have children identify speech marks in the text. Copy the text from pages 4–5 onto a piece of paper. Tell children to colour over the words that are between the speech marks. Have them role-play the conversation by reading the text between the speech marks.

Writing

- Have children draw a picture of their pet or a pet that they would like to own, and to write a description including what their pet looks like, what it likes to do and how they look after it.
- Turn to page 9 and ask, *What type of text is this?* Discuss the features and purpose of a letter. Have children write a letter to their parents or a friend.

▶ ELL engagement

- Collect pictures or soft toys of rabbits. Use these items to prompt a discussion about rabbits. Ask, *What do rabbits look like?* Help children in naming the different body parts of rabbits. Ask, *What covers the rabbit's body? How many legs do they have?* Discuss how they move and what sounds they make. Talk about where they live and what they do. Brainstorm and record on the board words associated with rabbits. Enlarge a copy of **PW 30** (page 50) onto A3 paper for each child and have them follow the instructions to make a rabbit. When finished, have children retell how they made their rabbit.

▶ Assessment

- PWs 28, 29 and 30 completed
- Note the child's responses, attempts and reading behaviours before, during and after reading
- Collect work samples, e.g. PW 28 could be kept in the child's portfolio
- Complete Running Record (page 130)

Name: ______________________ Date: ______________

Characters, setting and plot

You will need: coloured pencils

- Write about the **characters** in the story. Add a matching picture.
- Write about the **setting** of the story. Add a matching picture.
- Write about your favourite part of the **plot**. Add a matching picture.

Characters
Setting
Plot

Main teaching focus
Comprehension: Discussing the characters, setting and plot of a story.

Other teaching focus
Comprehension: Recalling information from a text.

Teacher's note
Children write about the characters, setting and plot of the story. Then they draw pictures in the boxes to match their writing.

Engage Literacy is published in 2013 by Raintree • *Lea Wants a Rabbit*, Level 17. This page may be photocopied for educational use within the purchasing institution.

Name: ______________________________ Date: _____________

Contractions

You will need: coloured pencils

- Draw lines to match the words to their contraction.

didn't	I will
that's	can not
where's	let us
let's	it is
I'm	did not
can't	do not
don't	where is
it's	I am
we'll	we will
there's	that is
I'll	there is

- Write the contraction to match the words.

that is ____________ I will ____________ do not ____________

did not ____________ where is ____________

- Write the words to match the contraction.

it's ____________ there's ____________ we'll ____________

I'm ____________ let's ____________ can't ____________

Main teaching focus
Word structures: Contractions.

Other teaching focus
Writing: Spelling contractions.

Teacher's note
Children draw a line to match the words to the contractions. Then they write the contractions to match the words and the words to match the contractions.

Engage Literacy is published in 2013 by Raintree • *Lea Wants a Rabbit*, Level 17. This page may be photocopied for educational use within the purchasing institution.

PW 30

Name: ______________________ Date: ____________

Make a rabbit

You will need: coloured pencils, scissors, glue, cotton wool, string

- Colour the parts of the rabbit.
- Cut them out and paste them together as shown.
- Paste some cotton wool onto your rabbit to make fur.
- Cut small pieces of string and paste them on your rabbit to make its whiskers.

Main teaching focus
Oral language development: Language and vocabulary development.

Other teaching focus
Oral language development: Retelling an experience.

Teacher's note
Children colour and cut out the parts. They paste them together and paste on cotton wool and string for the fur and whiskers. Children then retell how they made their rabbit.

Engage Literacy is published in 2013 by Raintree • *Lea Wants a Rabbit,* Level 17. This page may be photocopied for educational use within the purchasing institution.

Animals with Fins, Animals with Fur

Level 17 **Non-fiction** **Word count:** 349 **Text type:** Recount

HFW introduced: colour, hard, keep, keeps, spend, towards, warm, wish

HFW consolidated: about, busy, chasing, cool, enormous, everything, most, rolling, something, swim, week

Linking text: *Lea Wants a Rabbit* (fiction)

Curriculum link: pets/animals, school, environment, science

Phonic awareness: consonant digraph 'ph'; vowel digraphs 'ar', 'ou', 'ow'; split vowel digraphs 'i_e', 'a_e'; syllables; homophones 'too', 'to'

Text summary: Nick writes a letter to his Uncle Jarrad telling him about his school project.

Tuning in

- Ask children to think of animals that have fins. Record their ideas on the board. Have children role-play the movements of animals that have fins. Discuss how animals that have fins swim. Repeat for animals with fur. Talk about how animals with fur can live on land and some of them can also swim.

Book walk

- Introduce the text. Give each child a copy of the book and discuss the title. Ask children to share what they think the text will be about. Have children make predictions, using the title and cover pictures as prompts. Ask, *What do you think we will read about in this text? What animals might we learn about?* Link to the children's personal experiences.
- Flip through the book, discussing events and photographs. Promote language that is used throughout the text. Discuss how photographs help us to read the text. When questioning, use vocabulary from the text.

  pages 2–3: Ask, *What do you think Nick has done a school project about? Do you think he found out lots of things about animals with fins and animals with fur? Name some animals that have fins. How would fins help these animals in the water?*
  pages 4–5: Ask, *Can you see any little fins? Can fins be big? Which animal has fins that are enormous? What would help the animal swim fast and slow? What helps the animal swim towards food, or away from something that is chasing it? Do you think fins would help the animal turn?*
  pages 6–7: Ask, *What do these animals have covering their body? What does the fur look like? Do you think the fur helps to keep the animal warm when it is cold? Can fur be long? Can fur be short?*
  pages 8–9: Ask, *Which animal has fur that is soft? Why are rabbits good to hold? Would hedgehogs' fur make them good to hold?*
  pages 10–11: Ask, *Where do most animals with fur live? Do some animals with fur spend a lot of time in the water? How would thick fur help fur seals and otters in the water?*
  pages 12–13: Ask, *How does the colour of an animal's fur help it to hide? Where does a lion's fur help it to hide? How does the polar bear's fur make it hard to see on the ice? Why is it good that some foxes have white fur in winter and brown fur in summer?*
  pages 14–15: Ask, *What did Nick learn all about? If he is learning about volcanoes next week, do you think he should write another letter to Uncle Jarrad telling him about what he learns?*
  page 16: Ask, *Where did we see these words in the text? What do these words mean?* Discuss that the glossary shows us the meaning of words that are in the text. Read the words with the children and talk about what they mean.

Reading the text

- Have children read independently. Focus on meaning, structure and visual cues. Support development of reading strategies. Identify areas that challenge children and can be developed into future learning experiences.
- Discuss reading strategies. During reading, ask, *How could you work out this word? Did that make sense?*
- Ask children to relate the text to their own experiences. Ask, *What animals have you seen that have fins/fur? Where have you seen an animal that has fins/fur?*
- Ask children to summarise the main ideas in the text.
- Discuss how this is an information text that teaches readers about animals with fins and animals with fur. Ask, *What did you learn about by reading this text? What did you find out about animals with fins/fur?*
- Ask inferential questions such as: *How might a fish move if it didn't have fins? Why would a whale need big fins instead of small fins? How might a hedgehog's fur help to protect it? Does an animal's fur help it to survive?*

After reading

Focus on meaning, structure and visual cues that children found difficult while reading. Discuss strategies and provide opportunities for children to consolidate specific skills. For example, if children had difficulty with the word 'hedgehogs', discuss strategies such as sounding out the phonemes, re-reading, looking at the pictures or using the sentence content.

Choose from the following activities.

Comprehension

- *Answering literal questions:* As a group, discuss what children learnt about animals with fins and animals with fur. Write the literal question 'Do little fish have big fins or small fins?' on the board. Write the children's answer next to the question. Repeat with other literal questions, such as 'What type of fur do bats have?' or 'How does a lion's fur help it?' If children are unsure of the answer, discuss the strategy of answering literal questions by referring back to the text and finding the answer. Have children complete **PW 31** (page 53), answering literal questions.
- *Recall:* Have children sit in a circle and think of what they learnt about animals with fins and animals with fur. Move around the circle, asking each child to share something different that they learnt about animals with fins. Repeat for animals with fur. Have children complete **PW 32** (page 54), recording facts about animals with fins and animals with fur.

Phonological awareness

- Find 'dolphin' in the text and discuss the digraph 'ph'. Model the sound that these letters make together and discuss how it is the same sound as 'f'.
- Ask children to find 'shark' and talk about the sound made when the letters 'ar' are together. Talk about how 'shark' can be read by sounding 'sh-ar-k'. Have children think of and record other 'ar' words and underline the 'ar' in each word.
- Talk about split vowel digraphs and how the first vowel becomes a long vowel. Find 'time' and 'make' in the text and have children practise sounding them. Ask them to find other words in the text that have split vowel digraphs.
- As a group, clap the syllables in 'enormous'. Ask, *How many syllables are in this word?* Discuss the beginning, middle and ending sounds in the word. Count the number of syllables in other words from the text.
- Identify 'about' and discuss the vowel digraph 'ou'. Model the sound these letters make together. Ask children to count words with the 'ou' digraph in the text. Repeat for 'brown' and 'ow'. Discuss how the digraphs 'ou' and 'ow' can make the same sound.
- Explain that homophones are words that sound the same when they are read but they have different meanings. Have children find 'to' and 'too' in the text. Support them in discussing the meaning and use of these words by using the context of the sentences. Write the two words in other sentences on the board to model their meaning and use, e.g., 'It is too hot to go out.'

Vocabulary

- *Visual recognition of high-frequency words:* 'colour', 'hard', 'keep', 'keeps', 'spend', 'towards', 'warm', 'wish'. Ask children to find these words in the text. Write the words on cards (two cards for each word) and play games, such as Concentration and Snap.
- Ask children to write the high-frequency words in alphabetical order.

Fluency

- Discuss the importance of reading smoothly and without stopping. Demonstrate how to read fluently. Have children practise by reading the text to each other.

Text conventions

- *Features of the front cover:* Ask children to identify the title and author on the front cover. Explain that the author is the person who wrote the text. Ask, *What is the title? Who is the author?*
- *Features of the back cover:* Have children identify the blurb on the back cover. Discuss how we can read the blurb to get an idea of what the text will be about. Ask, *Does the blurb match what the text was about?*
- *Text type—letter:* Discuss how this text is a letter written from Nick to his Uncle Jarrad. Help children to identify the features of the letter.

Writing

- Have children write their own letter to a family member or friend explaining what they have been learning about at school. Ensure they include the features of a letter.

▸ ELL engagement

- Write 'Fins' at the top of a piece of paper and 'Fur' at the top of another. Ask, *What animals do we know that have fins/fur?* Record the animal names on the appropriate sheet of paper. Choose an animal from each category and ask, *How are these animals the same/different?* Have children complete **PW 33** (page 55), sorting animal pictures, and comparing and contrasting.

▸ Assessment

- PWs 31, 32 and 33 completed
- Note the child's responses, attempts and reading behaviours before, during and after reading
- Collect work samples, e.g. PW 31 could be kept in the child's portfolio
- Complete Running Record (page 131)

Name: ____________________ Date: ____________

Answering questions

- Write the answers to the questions on the lines.

1 What animal has enormous fins?

____

2 How do fins help an animal in the water?

____

3 What is an animal that has little fins?

____

4 When does fur help keep animals warm?

____

5 What is an animal that has very soft fur?

____

6 Where do most animals with fur live?

____

- List some animals that have fins and some animals that have fur.

Animals with fins	Animals with fur

Main teaching focus
Comprehension: Answering literal questions.

Other teaching focus
Comprehension: Recalling information from the text.

Teacher's note
Children write the answers to the questions. Then they list some animals that have fins and some animals that have fur.

Engage Literacy is published in 2013 by Raintree • *Animals with Fins, Animals with Fur,* Level 17. This page may be photocopied for educational use within the purchasing institution.

Name: ______________________ Date: ______________

Fins and fur

You will need: coloured pencils

- Write facts about animals with fins and animals with fur on the lines.
- Draw some animals with fins and animals with fur in the boxes.

Fins	**Some animals with fins**
______________________ ______________________ ______________________ ______________________ ______________________ ______________________ ______________________	
Fur	**Some animals with fur**
______________________ ______________________ ______________________ ______________________ ______________________ ______________________ ______________________	

Main teaching focus
Comprehension: Recalling information from a text.

Other teaching focus
Comprehension: Comparing and contrasting.

Teacher's note
Children recall facts from the text and record them in the 'Fins' and 'Fur' boxes. Then they draw pictures of animals with fins and animals with fur.

Engage Literacy is published in 2013 by Raintree • *Animals with Fins, Animals with Fur*, Level 17. This page may be photocopied for educational use within the purchasing institution.

Name: ______________________ Date: ____________

PW 33

Sorting animals

You will need: coloured pencils, scissors, glue, a piece of paper

- Colour and cut out the animals.
- Paste an animal with fins next to animal with fur on a piece of paper.
- Write two ways that they are the same and two ways that they are different.

Main teaching focus
Oral language: Language and vocabulary development.

Other teaching focus
Oral language: Comparing and contrasting.

Teacher's note
Children colour and cut out the pictures. They paste an animal with fins next to an animal with fur, then write two ways that the animals are the same and different. Then they continue with the other pictures.

Engage Literacy is published in 2013 by Raintree • *Animals with Fins, Animals with Fur*, Level 17. This page may be photocopied for educational use within the purchasing institution.

All About Teeth

Level 17 **Non-fiction** **Word count:** 386 **Text type:** Report

HFW introduced: begin, clean, hard, hardest, keep, part, same, stuck, talk
HFW consolidated: about, once, only, should
Linking text: *Wibbly Wobbly Tooth* (fiction)
Curriculum link: me/family, community
Phonic awareness: vowel digraphs 'ee', 'ew', 'ar'; split vowel digraph 'i_e'; root word 'all'; suffix 'ing'; antonyms
Text summary: Find out all about teeth! Learn what teeth look like, the different types of teeth and how they help us. Most importantly, learn how we can look after our teeth.

Tuning in

- Collect a toothbrush, toothpaste and dental floss and let children look at these items. Ask, *What are these things called? When do you use these things? Why do we brush our teeth?* Have children role-play the action of brushing their teeth.

Book walk

- Introduce the text. Give each child a copy of the book and discuss the title. Ask children to share what they think the text will be about. Have children make predictions, using the title and cover pictures as prompts. Have children predict if this is a fiction or a non-fiction text.
- Flip through the book, discussing events and pictures. Promote language that is used throughout the text. Discuss how pictures help us to read the text. When questioning, use vocabulary from the text.

pages 2–3: Ask, *How do your teeth help you? Do they help you eat food? Do they help you talk? Are all your teeth the same? Does this boy have any sharp teeth called incisors? How might these sharp teeth help you cut up food when you eat? Which teeth have flat tops? How do you think the molars help you chew food?*
pages 4–5: Ask, *Can you see all of your teeth or are parts of them hidden under your gum? Where is the top of the tooth? Where is the root? Where is the gum? Is the outside of your tooth very hard or soft? Why do you think the enamel is the hardest part of your body? What do you think the inside of your tooth is like? Why do you think the pulp is soft? Discuss the diagrams.*
pages 6–7: Ask, *Can you see the teeth of a tiny baby? Where are the baby's teeth growing? What happens when you are a bit older? Where do the teeth start to come out of? What do we call the first teeth you have? What is growing under your baby teeth? Why do you think they are called your second teeth?*
pages 8–9: Ask, *What happens to your baby teeth when you are about six or seven? Why do your baby teeth need to fall out? What comes out of your gums when your baby teeth have fallen out? How old do you think you would be when you have all 32 of your second teeth?*
pages 10–11: Ask, *What do you need to do so that you always have a lovely smile? When do you clean your teeth? What should you brush your teeth with? What parts of your teeth do you need to brush? Do you clean the top, front and back of your teeth? Do you need to brush every tooth? What do you do with the floss? Does the toothbrush get to the sides of your teeth?*
pages 12–13: Ask, *What type of food do you need to eat to make your teeth strong? Should you eat or drink a lot of sugar? Why not?*
pages 14–15: Ask, *Who do you need to see twice a year? What does the dentist check for? How will the dentist know if you are taking care of your teeth? Why do you need to look after your teeth?*
page 16: Ask, *Where did we see these words in the text? What do these words mean?* Discuss that the glossary shows us the meaning of words that are in the text. Read the words with the children and talk about what they mean.

Reading the text

- Have children read independently. Focus on meaning, structure and visual cues. Support development of reading strategies. Identify areas that challenge children and can be developed into future learning experiences.
- Discuss reading strategies. During reading, ask, *How could you work out this word? Did that make sense?*
- Ask children to relate the text to their own experiences. Ask, *How do you look after your teeth? Do you eat healthy foods to keep your teeth strong? Have you been to the dentist? How many second teeth do you have? Can you find your incisors?*
- Ask children to summarise the main ideas of the text.
- Discuss how this is an information text that teaches readers about teeth. Ask, *What did you learn about by reading this text?*
- Ask inferential questions such as: *How would the incisors help cut up food? Why does the outside of your teeth need to be very hard? What might happen if you don't brush your teeth twice every day? What might happen if you don't floss your teeth?*

After reading

Focus on meaning, structure and visual cues that children found difficult while reading. Discuss strategies and provide opportunities for children to consolidate specific skills. For example, if children had difficulty with the word 'hardest', discuss strategies such as sounding out the phonemes, re-reading, looking at the pictures or using the sentence content.

Choose from the following activities.

Comprehension

- *Recall:* Discuss how people have a different number of teeth depending on their age. Draw a picture of a baby with no teeth on the board and ask, *How many teeth would the baby have?* Draw a picture of a three-year-old's mouth (without the teeth) and ask, *What type of teeth would they have?* As a group, draw in the appropriate baby teeth. Draw a picture of a seven-year-old's mouth (without the teeth) and ask, *What would their teeth be like?* Discuss how they might have some gaps, and a combination of baby and second teeth. Draw some teeth on the picture. Draw a picture of an adult and ask, *What type of teeth would this person have?* As a group, draw in the appropriate second teeth. Have children complete **PW 34** (page 58).

Phonological awareness

- Find 'teeth' in the text and discuss the vowel digraph 'ee'. Model the sound that these letters make together. Find and record other 'ee' words in the text and have children circle the 'ee' digraph in each word. Repeat for 'ew' in 'chew', and have the group list other 'ew' words, then practise the list words.
- Find 'hard' in the text. Discuss the sound made by 'ar'. Talk about how 'hard' can be read by sounding 'h-ar-d'. Have children identify 'ar' words in the text and practise reading them. Brainstorm and record other 'ar' words.
- Explain about split vowel digraphs and how the first vowel becomes a long vowel. Find 'time' in the text and have children practise sounding it. Ask them to find other words in the text with split vowel digraphs.
- Discuss the consonant diagraph 'sh' and how these letters are sounded to make one sound. Talk about how 'sh' can be at the beginning, middle or end of words. Find 'sh' words in the text, and brainstorm and record other 'sh' words. Repeat for 'th' and 'teeth' and have children count the 'th' words in the text.
- Find 'all' in the text. Talk about how new words can be made by adding letters to the front of this word. Have children find the word 'fall'. Ask, *Can you see 'all' in this word?* Cover up the 'f' at the start of the word and have children identify the word 'all'. Discuss how new words can be made by adding letters to the end of a word as well. Identify and discuss the word 'called'. Brainstorm and record other 'all' words and have children underline 'all' in each word.
- Discuss the sound the letters 'ing' make together and talk about how this suffix is added to the end of words. Ask children to identify the 'ing' suffix in the text.
- Identify the antonyms 'front' and 'back' in the text. Discuss how antonyms are words that mean the opposite. Give children a piece of paper, and as a group, have them think of and record other antonyms (e.g. 'up'/'down', 'good'/'bad').

Vocabulary

- *Visual recognition of high-frequency words:* 'begin', 'clean', 'hard', 'hardest', 'keep', 'part', 'same', 'stuck', 'talk'. Ask children to find these words in the text. Write the words on cards (two cards for each word) and play games, such as Concentration and Snap.
- *Theme words—teeth:* As a group, list the 'teeth' words used in the text. Encourage children to look at the glossary to see the meanings of these words. Have children record these words, write a simple definition and draw a picture to show the meaning. If they are unsure of the meaning of any words, encourage them to use the sentence content or the glossary.

Fluency

- Discuss the importance of reading smoothly and without stopping. Demonstrate how to read fluently. Have children practise by reading the text to each other.

Text conventions

- *Titles:* Turn to page 2 and discuss how 'Your Teeth' is shown in large, bold font at the top of the page. Talk about how these words are similar to a title as they are telling readers what they are going to read about on these pages. Ask children to find other titles in this text.

Writing

- Give children four pieces of paper and ask them as a group to draw pictures to show the four things they need to do to look after their teeth. Have them complete **PW 35** (page 59), writing about and drawing the four ways to look after their teeth.

▶ ELL engagement

- Show children food packaging from a variety of foods. As a group, talk about which foods are healthy and which foods are not as good to eat all the time. Encourage children to sort and categorise the foods into two groups: healthy foods and sometimes foods. Ask, *Can you think of any other foods that would fit into these categories?* Have children complete **PW 36** (page 60), sorting foods into 'healthy' and 'sometimes foods'.

▶ Assessment

- PWs 34, 35 and 36 completed
- Note the child's responses, attempts and reading behaviours before, during and after reading
- Collect work samples, e.g. PW 34 could be kept in the child's portfolio
- Complete Running Record (page 132)

Name: ______________________ Date: ____________

Which teeth?

- Use the words from the box to label the pictures. You can use two words twice. Refer to pages 4–5 of the book to help you.

enamel	top of your tooth	pulp	gum	bone	root

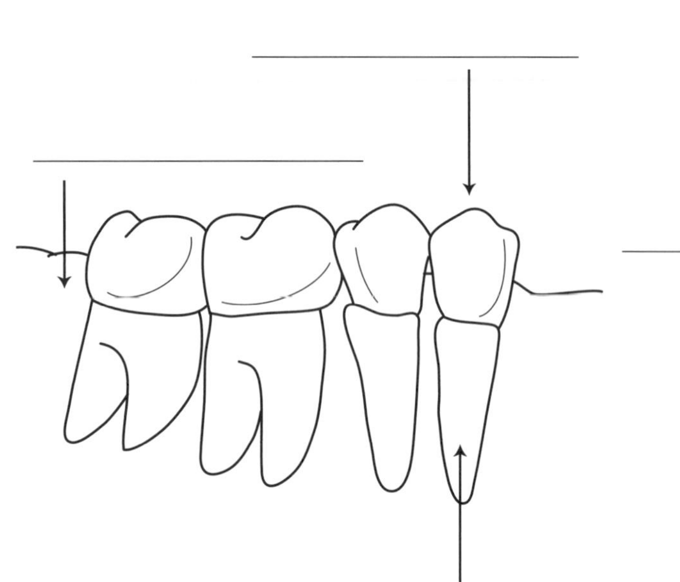

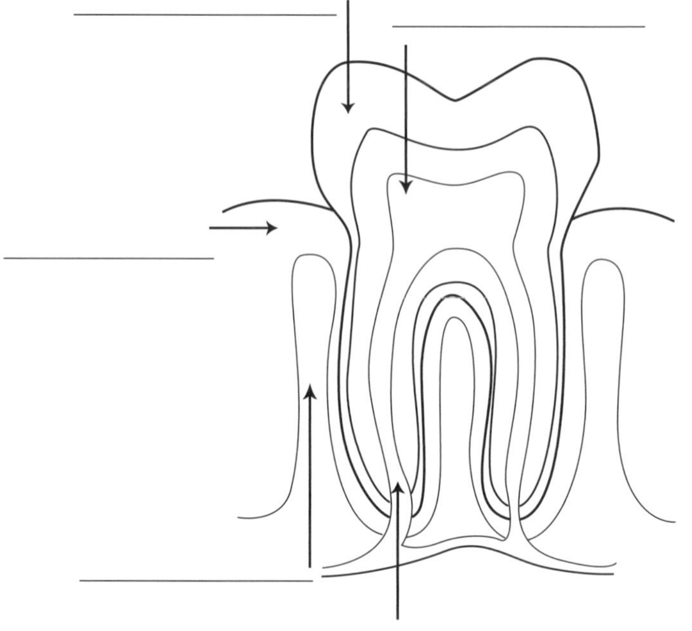

- Draw in some teeth in each person's mouth. Fill in the number you think they might have.

I am a baby.

I have _____ teeth.

I am seven years old.

I have _____ teeth.

Main teaching focus
Comprehension: Recalling information from the text.

Other teaching focus
Comprehension: Word meanings; definitions.

Teacher's note
Children label the parts of the diagrams using the words in the box. Then they draw some teeth in the mouth of the people. Children then complete the sentences, writing how many teeth a person of that age might have.

Engage Literacy is published in 2013 by Raintree • *All About Teeth*, Level 17. This page may be photocopied for educational use within the purchasing institution.

Name: ______________________ Date: ______________

How to look after your teeth

You will need: coloured pencils

- Write sentences about the four ways you can look after your teeth.
- Draw pictures to match your sentences. Use the book to help you.

Looking after your teeth

1 ________________	
2 ________________	
3 ________________	
4 ________________	

Main teaching focus
Writing: Writing an information report; including details in writing.

Other teaching focus
Comprehension: Recalling information from the text.

Teacher's note
Children write sentences explaining the four different ways to look after their teeth. Then they draw pictures to match their sentences.

Engage Literacy is published in 2013 by Raintree • *All About Teeth*, Level 17. This page may be photocopied for educational use within the purchasing institution.

Name: ______________________ Date: ______________

PW 36

Healthy foods

You will need: coloured pencils, scissors, glue, a piece of paper

- Colour and cut out the pictures.
- Sort the pictures into healthy foods and sometimes foods.
- Paste them on the paper in the two groups.

Main teaching focus
Oral language: Language and vocabulary development.

Other teaching focus
Comprehension: Comparing and contrasting.

Teacher's note
Children colour and cut out the pictures. Then they sort them into two categories—healthy foods and sometimes foods—and paste them in their groups on a piece of paper.

Engage Literacy is published in 2013 by Raintree • *All About Teeth*, Level 17. This page may be photocopied for educational use within the purchasing institution.

My Real Name IS Princess

Level 18 **Fiction** **Word count:** 435 **Text type:** Narrative

HFW introduced: beautiful, belong, carefully, disappeared, even, kindly, rush, sadly, special, surprise, unfolded

HFW consolidated: child, gold, happily, hard, listen, listened, placed, pretty, silver, stood, tried, while

Linking text: *Happy To Be Me* (non-fiction)

Curriculum link: me/family, school

Phonic awareness: suffixes 'ly', 'ed', 'ing'; prefix 'un'; syllables; split vowel digraphs 'a_e', 'i_e'; vowel digraphs 'oo', 'ou'; consonant phonemes 'll', 'bb', 'pp', 'ss'

Story summary: Princess doesn't feel like a real princess—that is, until she works really hard and writes a special story and Mrs Kay lets her wear the special cape!

Tuning in

- Talk about princesses. Give children a piece of paper and ask them to draw a picture of what they think a princess looks like. Have children share their pictures and ask, *What do princesses look like? What do princesses do? Where do princesses live?*

Book walk

- Introduce the story. Give each child a copy of the book and discuss the title. Ask children to share what they think the text will be about. Have children make predictions, using the title and cover illustration as prompts. Ask, *Who do you think Princess is? Can you see a princess on the front cover? What is the girl on the front cover doing? Why do you think the word 'IS' is shown in capital letters?* Have children predict if this is a fiction or a non-fiction text.
- Flip through the book, discussing events and illustrations. Promote language that is used throughout the text. Discuss how illustrations help us to read the text. When questioning, use vocabulary from the text.

pages 2–3: Ask, *Where are all the children sitting? Where is Mrs Kay? Can you see Bill, the big boy with red hair? Can you see a little girl in a spotty dress?*
pages 4–5: Ask, *Who do you think Princess might be? Why might Mrs Kay think Princess is not her real name? Do you think Princess feels like a princess? Does Princess look happy or sad?*
pages 6–7: Ask, *Where are the children sitting? What have they started to do? Are children reading with Mrs Kay? What is Princess beginning to write? What is her story about? Is Princess working hard? Does it look like she is rushing or taking her time? Do you think Princess likes writing stories? How does Princess feel now?*
pages 8–9: Ask, *What are the children doing now? What colour box has Mrs Kay brought out of her office? What is the surprise she has for them? What colour paper was in the box? What has Mrs Kay taken out of the box? What colour is the cape? What colour stars are all over the cape?*
pages 10–11: Ask, *Who does the cape belong to? Who wants to put on Mrs Kay's special cape and take it home for one week?*
pages 12–13: Ask, *Who was working very hard all morning? Who wrote a special story and tried her best? Who is Mrs Kay going to give the cape to?*
pages 14–15: Ask, *Who did Mrs Kay take the cape over to? Where did she place the cape? How did she tie up the cape? Is Princess smiling? Do you think she feels beautiful?*
page 16: Ask, *What are all the children doing? Who is Mrs Kay smiling at? Do you think Princess feels like a princess now?*

Reading the text

- Have children read independently. Focus on meaning, structure and visual cues. Support development of reading strategies. Identify areas that challenge children and can be developed into future learning experiences.
- Discuss reading strategies. During reading, ask, *How could you work out this word? Did that make sense?*
- Ask children to relate the text to their own experiences. Ask, *Have you ever worked hard on something at school? Have you ever had a reward for doing good work?*
- Have children retell the story in their own words.
- Talk about the characters, setting and plot.
- Discuss how this is a narrative text and talk about the features of narrative text.
- Ask inferential questions such as: *Why do you think Mrs Kay didn't think Princess was her real name? What made Princess feel like a real princess? Why do you think writing stories makes Princess feel happy?*

After reading

Focus on meaning, structure and visual cues that children found difficult while reading. Discuss strategies and provide opportunities for children to consolidate specific skills. For example, if children had difficulty with the word 'beautiful', discuss strategies such as sounding out the phonemes, re-reading, looking at the illustrations or using the sentence content.

Choose from the following activities.

Comprehension

- *Sequencing:* Have children talk about the events in the text. Flip through the text and ask children to explain what was happening in that part of the story. Give each child a piece of paper and ask them each to draw a different part of the story. When they have finished, ask them to share their picture with the group. Have children sequence their pictures in the correct order. As a group, write captions under the pictures. Have children complete **PW 37** (page 63), sequencing pictures and sentences.
- *Inferential questions:* Encourage children to think about the characters. Ask, *How did the characters feel during the story?* Discuss with children how when they answer questions about a story, sometimes they can find the answer in the text and sometimes they need to think about the characters and story to answer the question. Have children complete **PW 38** (page 64), inferring Princess's feelings.

Phonological awareness

- Identify the word 'slowly' in the text and talk about the 'ly' suffix. Discuss how 'ly' on the end of a word means that the word is telling us how something is being done. Repeat for the 'ed' and 'ing' suffixes.
- Find 'unfolded' and discuss the prefix 'un'. Talk about how prefixes are added to the front of words and they change the meaning of the word. Discuss how 'un' at the front of the word means 'not'. Ask children to brainstorm 'un' words. Record these words and discuss how their meaning is changed from the root word.
- As a group, clap the syllables in 'beautiful'. Ask, *How many syllables are in this word?* Discuss the beginning, middle and ending sounds in the word. Clap and count the number of syllables in other words from the text.
- Talk about split vowel digraphs and how the first vowel is a long vowel. Find 'like' and 'name' in the text and have children practise sounding them. Ask them to find other words in the text that have split vowel digraphs.
- Talk about the vowel digraph 'oo'. Find 'good' in the text and model the short sound the digraph makes in this word. Discuss the word 'room'. Talk about how the 'oo' vowel digraph in this word makes a long sound. Have children find other 'oo' words in the text and identify if they make a long sound or a short sound.
- Talk about the vowel digraph 'ou' in 'about'. Discuss the sound these letters make when they are together. Brainstorm and record other 'ou' words.
- Have children identify words in the text that have the double consonants 'll', 'bb', 'pp' and 'ss'. Discuss that, when there are double letters in a word, it is only one phoneme. Have children write the words with double consonants from the text, circle the double consonants and sound out the words.

Vocabulary

- *Visual recognition of high-frequency words:* 'beautiful', 'belong', 'carefully', 'disappeared', 'even', 'kindly', 'rush', 'sadly', 'special', 'surprise', 'unfolded'. Ask children to find these words in the text. Write the words on cards (two cards for each word) and play games, such as Concentration and Snap.
- Talk about the adjectives in the text. Explain how adjectives are describing words. Find the phrase 'big boy' on page 3 and ask, *What type of boy is he?* Discuss how the word 'big' is an adjective because it describes the boy. Have children find other adjectives in the text. Have children complete **PW 39** (page 65), drawing pictures to show the meaning of adjectives.

Fluency

- Discuss the importance of reading smoothly and without stopping. Demonstrate how to read fluently. Have children practise by reading the text to each other.

Text conventions

- *Features of the front cover:* Look at the front cover and ask children to identify the title, author and illustrator. Explain that the author wrote the text and the illustrator drew the pictures.
- *Features of the back cover:* As a group, look at the back cover and have children identify the blurb. Discuss how readers can read the blurb to get an idea of what the text will be about. Ask, *Does the blurb match what the text was about?*

Writing

- Ask children to draw a picture of a time when they felt like a princess/prince or a time when they were proud of themselves. Have them write sentences explaining what happened and how they felt.

▸ ELL engagement

- Show children pictures of castles. Ask, *Where do princesses, princes, kings and queens live?* Have children describe and label the parts of the castles. Focus on developing their language and language skills. Give children cardboard boxes, craft paper, newspapers, masking tape and glue. As a group, have them design and build a castle. When completed, ask children to retell the process of building the castle.

▸ Assessment

- PWs 37, 38 and 39 completed
- Note the child's responses, attempts and reading behaviours before, during and after reading
- Collect work samples, e.g. PW 37 could be kept in the child's portfolio
- Complete Running Record (page 133)

Name: ______________________ Date: ______________

Sequence and match

You will need: coloured pencils, scissors, glue, a strip of paper

- Colour and cut out the pictures. Cut out the groups of sentences.
- Match the groups of sentences to the pictures.
- Paste them onto paper in the correct order.

Princess got her book, too. Her story was all about a little girl who loved to dance.	"My name is Princess," said the little girl. "Oh, no, my dear," smiled Mrs Kay kindly. "What's your **real** name?"
"Well," said Mrs Kay, "it's Princess. Her story is very special and she has tried her best today."	Mrs Kay unfolded the paper and took out a pretty red cape. The cape had beautiful silver and gold stars all over it.

Main teaching focus
Comprehension: Sequencing events from the text.

Other teaching focus
Comprehension: Matching sentences with pictures.

Teacher's note
Children colour and cut out the pictures. They cut out the sentences. They match the pictures to the sentences and paste the pictures and sentences on a strip of paper in the correct order.

Engage Literacy is published in 2013 by Raintree • *My Real Name IS Princess*, Level 18. This page may be photocopied for educational use within the purchasing institution.

Name: ______________________________ Date: ______________

PW 38

How does Princess feel?

- Write the answers to the questions on the lines.

Why does Princess only feel like a princess sometimes?

____

Why do you think writing stories makes Princess feel happy?

____

Why does Princess feel like a real princess
when she has the cape on?

____

- Look at the pictures and write how Princess would have been feeling at that time. Write why she would have been feeling that way.

____

____

____

____

____

____

Main teaching focus
Comprehension: Drawing inferences from sentences.

Other teaching focus
Comprehension: Inferring a character's feelings.

Teacher's note
Children write the answer to the questions on the lines. Then they look at the pictures and write how Princess was feeling at different parts of the story.

Engage Literacy is published in 2013 by Raintree • *My Real Name IS Princess*, Level 18. This page may be photocopied for educational use within the purchasing institution.

Name: ______________________ Date: ____________

Adjectives

You will need: coloured pencils

- Draw pictures to show the meaning of the adjectives.

big boy	*red* hair	*little* girl
spotty dress	*blue* box	*green* paper
red cape	*silver* stars	*gold* stars
star cape	*red* dress	*beautiful* stars

Main teaching focus
Comprehension: Visualising adjectives.

Other teaching focus
Comprehension: Gaining meaning from text.

Teacher's note
Children read the phrases and draw a picture to show the meaning of the adjectives.

Engage Literacy is published in 2013 by Raintree • *My Real Name IS Princess*, Level 18. This page may be photocopied for educational use within the purchasing institution.

Snorkelling with Nana

Level 18 **Fiction** **Word count:** 437 **Text type:** Narrative

HFW introduced: against, anymore, beautiful, carefully, colourful, favourite, glad, knocked, know, sadly, such, visit

HFW consolidated: begged, okay, pretty, pushed, towards, tried, while

Linking text: *Underwater World* (non-fiction)

Curriculum link: family/me, physically active, environment

Phonic awareness: suffixes 'ed', 'ly'; alliteration; split vowel digraphs 'a_e', 'i_e'; contractions 'you're', 'don't'; vowel digraphs 'ea', 'aw'

Story summary: Gil has always wanted to go snorkelling with Nana. Then Nana takes Gil into the water, but he is scared by a big wave. Luckily, Gil is brave enough to try again and see the beautiful fish.

Tuning in

- Show children a snorkel, mask and flippers. Ask, *What are these called? What do you do with them?* Have children try them on. Ask, *How does it feel when you wear these things?* Have children role-play the action of snorkelling.

Book walk

- Introduce the story. Give each child a copy of the book and discuss the title. Ask children to share what they think the story will be about. Have children make predictions, using the title and cover illustration as prompts. Ask, *What are they doing? What would you see when you are snorkelling?* Have children predict if this is a fiction or a non-fiction text.
- Flip through the book, discussing events and illustrations. Promote language that is used throughout the text. Discuss how illustrations help us to read the text. When questioning, use vocabulary from the text.

  pages 2–3: Ask, *Where do Gil's Nana and Grandpa live? What does Grandpa love to do? Who do you think loves to find pretty shells? What else do you think Nana might love to do? Do you think Gil wants Nana to teach him how to snorkel every time he visits? Is Gil old enough to snorkel?*
  pages 4–5: Ask, *What do you think Gil asked Nana when he turned eight years old? Do you think Nana said 'yes' now that Gil is older and he is a good swimmer?*
  pages 6–7: Ask, *Where do Nana, Grandpa and Gil walk down to? What have they taken out to go snorkelling? Who is helping Gil to get ready? What has Grandpa got out?*
  pages 8–9: Ask, *Did Nana and Gil walk carefully into the water? What sound did their flippers make? What might happen when the big wave rolls in?*
  pages 10–11: Ask, *Did Gil get a fright? Do you think he likes snorkelling anymore? What would he be scared of? Would Nana want him to give up? Where could Gil play where he won't be scared while Nana goes and looks at the fish?*
  pages 12–13: Ask, *What has Gil taken off? What has he put on his head? What is he building? Where has Nana popped up? Who is waving at Gil? Does it look like Nana is having fun? Has Gil changed his mind? What has Gil put back on? Whose hand is Gil holding as he walks back into the sea?*
  pages 14–15: Ask, *Did Gil go back to Grandpa when the big wave came this time? Whose hand do you think he holds when the big wave comes? What are they swimming towards? Is Gil having fun? Can Gil see lots of beautiful fish next to the little rocks? What did they see when they were snorkelling for a long time?*
  page 16: Ask, *Do you think Gil is glad that he tried again even though he was scared? Would Nana be glad that he tried again? Who will always go snorkelling with Nana now?*

Reading the text

- Have children read independently. Focus on meaning, structure and visual cues. Support development of reading strategies. Identify areas that challenge children and can be developed into future learning experiences.
- Discuss reading strategies. During reading, ask, *How could you work out this word? Did that make sense?*
- Ask students to relate the text to their own experiences. Ask, *Have you ever been snorkelling or seen snorkelling on TV? What do you like to do at the beach? Have you been scared of something before? When is a time when you had to try again?*
- Have children retell the story in their own words.
- Talk about the characters, setting and plot.
- Discuss how this is a narrative text and talk about the features of narrative text.
- Ask inferential questions such as: *Why did Nana wait until Gil was a good swimmer before she took him snorkelling? Why do you think Gil decided to try again? Why would Gil be proud of himself?*

After reading

Focus on meaning, structure and visual cues that children found difficult while reading. Discuss strategies and provide

opportunities for children to consolidate specific skills. For example, if children had difficulty with the word 'beautiful', discuss strategies such as sounding out the phonemes, re-reading, looking at the illustrations or using the sentence content.

Choose from the following activities.

Comprehension

- *Story map:* Have children recall what happened in the story. Ask, *What happened at the beginning/middle/end?* Encourage children to role-play the events, focusing on the sequence. Draw six large boxes on the board. Ask, *What happened first?* In the first box, draw a picture of Gil visiting Nana and Grandpa and asking Nana if he could go snorkelling. Repeat until the events of the story have been recorded in the boxes. Draw arrows between the boxes to show the sequence of events. Have children complete **PW 40** (page 68), drawing pictures in sequence.
- *Recall:* Ask, *What characters were in the story? Where did the story take place? What happened in the story?* Give children a piece of paper and have them draw a picture of the setting, characters and their favourite part of the plot. Ask children to share and explain their drawing to the group.
- *Synonyms:* Find the phrase 'small house' on page 2. Talk about how 'small' means the same as 'little', and how 'small house' would mean the same as 'little house'. Explain how 'small' and 'little' are synonyms because they have the same meaning. Write the phrase 'pretty shells' on the board and ask, *Can anyone think of a synonym for the word 'pretty'?* Discuss how 'beautiful shells' would mean the same as 'pretty shells'. Choose other words in the text for children to think of synonyms for. Have children complete **PW 41** (page 69), writing synonyms to match words.

Phonological awareness

- Talk about the suffix 'ed' and how it can be added to the end of words. Have children find words in the text that end with 'ed' and practise reading them. Talk about how 'ed' on the end of a word means it has already happened (i.e. past tense). Repeat for 'ly'.
- Focus on the alliteration in the phrase 'Flip! Flop! Flip! Flop!' on page 8. Talk about how all the words start with the same sound, and that they sound good when read together.
- Talk about split vowel digraphs and how the first vowel is a long vowel. Find 'came' and 'time' in the text and have children practise sounding them. Ask them to find other words in the text that have split vowel digraphs.
- Find 'you're' in the text. Write 'you are' and 'you're' on the board and discuss how the contraction has an apostrophe instead of the letter 'a'. Repeat for the contraction 'don't'. Have children find the contractions in the text.
- Find 'sea' in the text. Identify the vowel digraph 'ea' and model the sound that these letters make together. Have children find other 'ea' words in the text.
- Talk about the vowel digraph 'aw'. Discuss the sound that these letters make together. Find 'saw' in the text and have children sound the word as 's-aw' to emphasise the 'aw' digraph. Brainstorm other words that end with 'aw'.

Vocabulary

- *Visual recognition of high-frequency words:* 'against', 'anymore', 'beautiful', 'carefully', 'colourful', 'favourite', 'glad', 'knocked', 'know', 'sadly', 'such', 'visit'. Ask children to find these words in the text. Write the words on cards (two cards for each word) and play games, such as Concentration and Snap.
- Have children write the high-frequency words in a sentence.

Fluency

- Discuss the importance of reading smoothly and without stopping. Demonstrate how to read fluently. Have children practise by reading the text to each other.

Text conventions

- *Commas:* As a group, discuss commas and have children identify the commas in the text. Talk about how readers pause at a comma when they are reading. Model this to children and then have them practise, using the text.
- *Exclamation marks:* Talk about how exclamation marks are used to show something is important or exciting and they influence the way the text is read. Have children identify the exclamation marks in the text. Ask them to practise reading the sentences with exclamation marks and then compare how they would be read without exclamation marks.

Writing

- Have children write a text about what they like to do at the beach. Brainstorm words that they might use in their writing and have those words available for children to refer to while writing. Support children in using details in their writing and encourage them to use adjectives.

▸ ELL engagement

- Encourage children to retell the events of the story. Have them make puppets using **PW 42** (page 70). Ask children to use the puppets to retell the story. Support and enhance children's language use during the activity.

▸ Assessment

- PWs 40, 41 and 42 completed
- Note the child's responses, attempts and reading behaviours before, during and after reading
- Collect work samples, e.g. PW 28 could be kept in the child's portfolio
- Complete Running Record (page 134)

Name: ______________________ Date: ______________

Story map

You will need: coloured pencils

- Draw pictures in the boxes to show the order of what happened in the story.

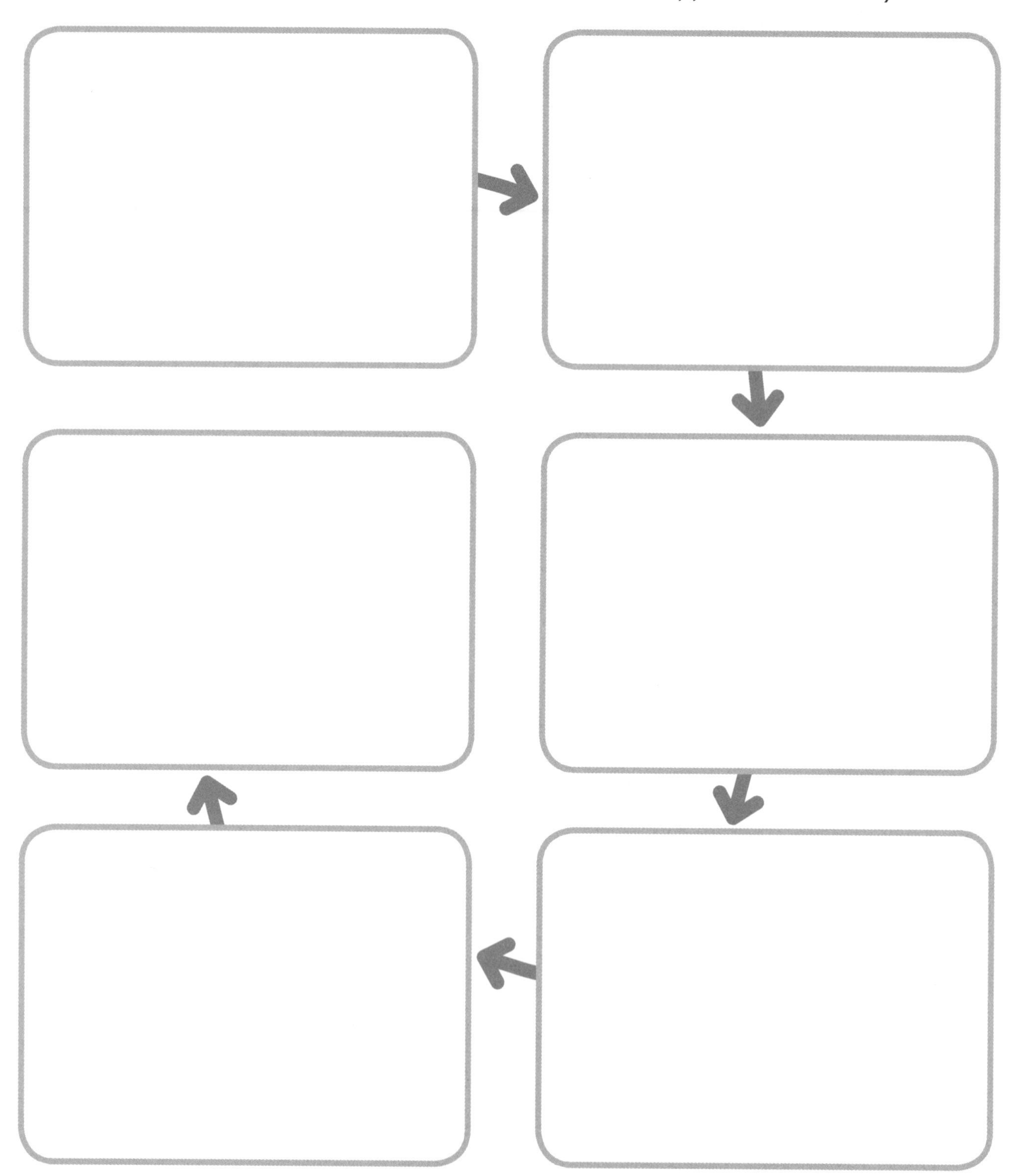

Main teaching focus
Comprehension: Sequencing events from the text.

Other teaching focus
Comprehension: Recalling events from the text.

Teacher's note
Children draw pictures in the boxes to show the sequence of events in the story.

Engage Literacy is published in 2013 by Raintree • *Snorkelling with Nana*, Level 18. This page may be photocopied for educational use within the purchasing institution.

Name: ______________________ Date: ______________

Synonyms

You will need: coloured pencils

- Think of a synonym for the underlined word.
- Rewrite the sentence using the synonym.
- Draw pictures in the boxes to show the meaning of the sentences.

Nana loved to find <u>pretty</u> shells.

____

____

Gil's Nana and Grandpa lived in a <u>small</u> house.

____

____

A <u>big</u> wave rolled in and knocked Gil over.

____

____

"No!" said Gil. "I'm too <u>scared</u>."

____

____

"Let's swim towards the <u>little</u> rocks," smiled Nana.

____

____

Main teaching focus
Comprehension: Synonyms; paraphrasing.

Other teaching focus
Comprehension: Gaining meaning from text.

Teacher's note
Children think of a synonym for the underlined word in each sentence. Then they rewrite the sentence using the synonym. Children draw a picture to match the sentence.

Engage Literacy is published in 2013 by Raintree • *Snorkelling with Nana,* Level 18. This page may be photocopied for educational use within the purchasing institution.

Name: ______________________ Date: ____________

PW 42

Puppets

You will need: coloured pencils, scissors, tape, craft sticks

- Colour and cut round the pictures.
- Use tape to stick a craft stick to the back of each picture.

Main teaching focus
Comprehension: Role-playing events of the story.
Oral language: Developing language and vocabulary.

Other teaching focus
Comprehension: Retelling events of the story.

Teacher's note
Children colour and cut out the pictures. Then they make puppets by taping a craft stick to the back of each picture.

Engage Literacy is published in 2013 by Raintree • *Snorkelling with Nana*, Level 18. This page may be photocopied for educational use within the purchasing institution.

Happy To Be Me

Level 18 **Non-fiction** **Word count:** 417 **Text type:** Exposition

HFW introduced: beautiful, because, I've, know, mine, special, thought, throw, until, upset

HFW consolidated: fastest, great, hard, keep, same, tried, trying, wanted, wants

Linking text: *My Real Name IS Princess* (fiction)

Curriculum link: me/family, school, community, celebrations

Phonic awareness: split digraphs 'a_e', 'o_e'; vowel digraphs 'aw', 'ow', 'ar', 'er'; suffixes 'er', 's', 'ed', 'ing', 'est'; contractions 'can't', 'don't'

Text summary: Jack writes a letter to his friend Amy, explaining that she shouldn't be upset that she isn't a good dancer. Jack reminds her of the things that she can do really well!

Tuning in

- Have children show you a happy expression. Ask them to describe what a happy face is like and record words such as 'smile' and 'grin'. Have children show you a sad expression. Ask them to describe what a sad face is like and record words such as 'frown', 'upset', 'crying' and 'tears'. Ask, *What things make you happy/sad?*

Book walk

- Introduce the text. Give each child a copy of the book and discuss the title. Ask children to share what they think the story will be about. Ask, *What does 'Happy To Be Me' mean? What is the boy holding? Why might he have a letter? Does the boy look happy or sad?*
- Have children read the blurb on the back cover. Ask, *Now that you have read the blurb, what do you think the text will be about?*
- Flip through the book, discussing events and illustrations. Promote language that is used throughout the text. Discuss how illustrations help us to read the text. When questioning, use vocabulary from the text.

  pages 2–3: Ask, *How do you think Amy felt when a girl said she was not good at dancing? Do you think she would be good at other things? Is Amy the best piano player in the class? Do you think she would be good at swimming and drawing? What should Amy do if she finds dancing hard?*
  pages 4–5: Ask, *What does Jack find hard? Why do you think Jack thinks about what he is good at while he is doing his maths? Who helps Jack with his maths after school?*
  pages 6–7: Ask, *What else does Jack get upset about? How did Jack feel when a boy said he had funny hair? Why might Mum have said it's a good thing that we don't all look the same?*
  pages 8–9: Ask, *Would Amy be good at other things even though she finds dancing hard? Are her drawings beautiful? Are Jack drawings as good as Amy's? Could Amy help Jack with drawing? Could Jack help Amy with her dancing?*
  pages 10–11: Ask, *Is everybody good at something? Does everyone find something hard? Would Jack's teacher be good at everything? What does Mr Grant find hard? What did he have to do with the bad cake that he made?*
  pages 12–13: Ask, *What is Sam sitting in? Do you think he can play sport? Why might people think that he can't play sport? Is Sam good at basketball? Does he get goals? Do you think everyone wants Sam on their team?*
  pages 14–15: Ask, *What could Amy do when she is feeling sad? Should everybody be happy with who they are? Do you think Jack thinks Amy is a special friend?*
  page 16: Ask, *Where did we see these words in the text? What do these words mean?* Discuss that the glossary shows us the meaning of words that are in the text. Read through the words and talk about what they mean.

Reading the text

- Have children read independently. Focus on meaning, structure and visual cues. Support development of reading strategies. Identify areas that challenge children and can be developed into future learning experiences.
- Ask children to relate the text to their own experiences. Ask, *Have you ever been upset about something you weren't good at? What are you good at?*
- Have children retell the text in their own words.
- Talk about the purpose of the text. Ask, *What do we learn by reading this text?*
- Ask inferential questions such as: *Why do you think Jack wrote a letter to Amy? How do you think Amy will feel after she reads the letter? What other things could Jack do to help Amy feel better? Why is Jack a good friend?*

After reading

Focus on meaning, structure and visual cues that children found difficult while reading. Discuss strategies and provide opportunities for children to consolidate specific skills. For example, if children had difficulty with the word 'dancing', discuss strategies such as sounding out the phonemes, re-reading, looking at the illustrations or using the sentence content.

Choose from the following activities.

Comprehension

- *Recall:* Have children discuss the events of the text. Ask, *What was Jack explaining to Amy in the letter? What did he want Amy to realise?* Talk about the things that the characters in the text were good at. Write 'Jack' on the board and next to his name have children draw the things he is good at and the things he finds hard. Repeat for Amy, Mr Grant and Sam. Have children complete **PW 43** (page 73), identifying what the characters are good at.

Phonological awareness

- Talk about split vowel digraphs and how the first vowel is a long vowel. Find 'cake' and 'home' in the text and have children practise sounding them. Ask them to find other words in the text that have split vowel digraphs.
- Find 'draw' in the text. Discuss the vowel digraph 'aw' and have children practise sounding these letters together. Ask them to brainstorm other words that end with the 'aw' digraph.
- Discuss the vowel digraph 'ow'. Have children find 'throw' in the text and discuss how the phonemes are sounded as 'th-r-ow'. Talk about the sound made by 'ow' in 'throw'.
- Find 'hard' in the text. Discuss the sound made when the letters 'ar' are together. Talk about how 'hard' can be read by sounding 'h-ar-d'. Brainstorm and record other 'ar' words.
- Find 'brother' in the text and discuss the sound made when the letters 'er' are together. Have children find 'er' words in the text and have them practise reading them.
- Talk about how the suffix 'er' can be added to the end of words. Talk about how 'er' on the end of a word lets us know what someone is doing. Write 'teach' on the board and ask children to read the word and talk about the meaning. Add 'er' to the end to make 'teacher'. Discuss how 'teacher' refers to someone who is teaching. Ask children to find words with the suffix 'er' in the text. Have children complete **PW 44** (page 74), making and using 'er' words.
- Talk about the suffixes 's', 'ed' and 'ing'. Discuss how each of these suffixes can be added to the end of words and that they can change the tense of the word. Have children find words with these suffixes in the text.
- Find 'fastest' in the text and identify the suffix 'est'. Explain that the 'est' suffix means that something is the most. Discuss the meaning of 'fastest'.
- Find 'can't' in the text. Write 'cannot' and 'can't' on the board and discuss how the contraction has an apostrophe instead of the letters 'no'. Repeat for 'don't'. Have children find the contractions in the text.

Vocabulary

- *Visual recognition of high-frequency words:* 'beautiful', 'because', 'I've', 'know', 'mine', 'special', 'thought', 'throw', 'until', 'upset'. Ask children to find these words in the text. Write the words on cards (two cards for each word) and play games, such as Concentration and Snap.
- Have children write the high-frequency words in bubble writing using coloured pencils. Encourage children to focus on recognising the letter patterns in the words.

Fluency

- Discuss the importance of reading smoothly and without stopping. Demonstrate how to read fluently. Have children practise by reading the text to each other.

Text conventions

- *Text emphasis/italic font:* Talk about how some words in the text are shown in italics. Discuss that this is because they are words that children might not recognise. Show children how we can find the meaning of the words by looking at the glossary on page 16.
- *Text type—letter:* Discuss how this text is a letter written from Jack to his friend Amy. Help children to identify the features of the letter in the text.

Writing

- Have each child think about what they are good at and what things they find hard. Ask them to share their ideas with a partner. Ask, *Was anybody good at the same things? Were people good at different things? Did anybody find the same things hard?* Discuss things you can do when you feel upset or if you find things difficult. Have children complete **PW 45** (page 75), recording what things they are good at and what things they find hard.

▶ ELL engagement

- Discuss why Jack is a good friend to Amy. Ask, *What makes a good friend?* As a group, make a list of things that good friends do. Discuss how friends help each other, are kind to each other, share, listen and play together. Encourage children to role-play different situations where they can be a good friend. During these discussions, focus on enhancing children's language development. Give children strips of paper and glue and have them make a friendship chain. On the strips of paper, have children write or draw their friends or nice things that they can do for their friends. Roll, link and paste the strips of paper together to make a paper chain. Ask, *What things will you do to be a good friend to the people on the friendship chain?*

▶ Assessment

- PWs 43, 44 and 45 completed
- Note the child's responses, attempts and reading behaviours before, during and after reading
- Collect work samples, e.g. PW 43 could be kept in the child's portfolio
- Complete Running Record (page 135)

Name: ______________________ Date: ______________

Who was good at ...?

You will need: scissors, glue

- Write the answer to the question.

What can you do if you aren't very good at something?

____

____

- Cut out the words in the boxes below. Match them with the right character.

I am good at ...

I need to keep trying at ...

basketball	drawing	running
cooking	dancing	maths

Main teaching focus
Comprehension: Recalling information from the text.

Other teaching focus
Comprehension: Drawing inferences from a sentence by reasoning.

Teacher's note
Children answer the question on the lines. Children cut out the words, and match and paste them with the appropriate characters.

Engage Literacy is published in 2013 by Raintree • *Happy To Be Me*, Level 18. This page may be photocopied for educational use within the purchasing institution.

Name: ______________________ Date: ______________

‘er’ words

- Add ‘er’ to the end of the words.
- Draw a line to match the words to the pictures.

piano play __ __

bak __ __

runn __ __

danc __ __

teach __ __

basketball play __ __

- Write these ‘er’ words in a sentence.

dancer ____

____

teacher ____

____

runner ____

____

- What other ‘er’ words can you think of?

______________ ______________ ______________

______________ ______________ ______________

Main teaching focus
Phonological awareness: Vowel before ‘r’—‘er’.

Other teaching focus
Writing: Sounding unknown words using familiar letter patterns; writing simple and complex sentences.

Teacher’s note
Children add ‘er’ to the words and draw a line to match the words to the pictures. Children write the ‘er’ words in a sentence. Then they think of and record other ‘er’ words.

Engage Literacy is published in 2013 by Raintree • *Happy To Be Me*, Level 18. This page may be photocopied for educational use within the purchasing institution.

Name: ______________________ Date: ______________

What am I good at?

You will need: coloured pencils

- Draw your face in the head.

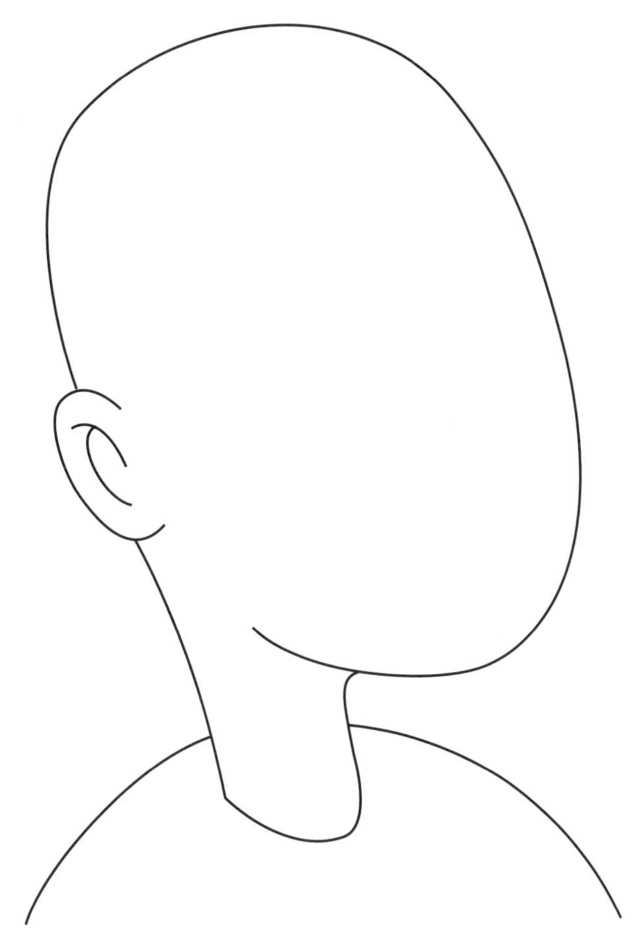

- Make a list of things you are good at.
- Make a list of things you find hard.

Things I am good at ...	Things I find hard ...
______________________	______________________
______________________	______________________
______________________	______________________

Main teaching focus
Oral language: Developing language and vocabulary.

Other teaching focus
Comprehension: Linking text to personal experiences; comparing and contrasting.

Teacher's note
Children draw their face in the outline of the head. Then they write a list of things they think they are good at and the things they find hard in the appropriate space.

Engage Literacy is published in 2013 by Raintree • *Happy To Be Me*, Level 18. This page may be photocopied for educational use within the purchasing institution.

Underwater World

Level 18 **Non-fiction** **Word count:** 439 **Text type:** Report

HFW introduced:	beautiful, because, carefully, colourful, know, smaller, smallest, such
HFW consolidated:	bright, colours, full, hard, many, part, spend, warm
Linking text:	*Snorkelling with Nana* (fiction)
Curriculum link:	environment, science, animals
Phonic awareness:	vowel digraphs 'ay', 'ea', 'aw', 'ar'; vowel trigraph 'igh'; antonyms; split digraphs 'a_e', 'i_e'; consonant digraphs 'th', 'sh'
Text summary:	Learn about the beautiful world under the sea that is full of plants and animals.

Tuning in

- As a group, make a list of plants and animals that live underwater in the sea. Have children role-play the movements of different sea animals. Ask, *What big/small things live underwater?*

Book walk

- Introduce the text. Give each child a copy of the book and discuss the title. Ask children to share what they think the text will be about. Ask, *What would an underwater world be like? What animals can you see that live underwater? What plants can you see that live underwater?*
- Have children read the blurb on the back cover. Ask, *Now that you have read the blurb, what do you think the text will be about?*
- Flip through the book, discussing events and photographs. Promote language that is used throughout the text. Discuss how photographs help us to read the text. When questioning, use vocabulary from the text.

pages 2–3: Ask, *What is in the beautiful world under the sea? Are there some animals and plants that are very small? Do you need to look carefully to see these animals and plants? What enormous animals and plants can you see here?*
pages 4–5: Ask, *Is the ocean home to lots of fish? Do fish live in warm/cold water? Are fish bright and colourful? What shape are fish? Can fish be big/small? Is the whale shark the biggest fish in the ocean? Do you think the smallest fish is smaller than a pea?*
pages 6–7: Ask, *What else lives in this underwater world? What do turtles have on their back? Is their shell hard or soft? Is their shell made of bone? Do turtles spend a lot of time under the water? Do they come to the top to breathe? Do turtles spend time on land? Where do they lay their eggs? Do they live for a long time?*
pages 8–9: Ask, *What else lives in the ocean? Where can you see lots of seaweed and seagrass? Where would these tiny animals called polyps live?* Identify the coral in the photo and explain how polyps make a house around themselves made of limestone. Explain how the polyps stay in one place. Ask, *What colour is coral? Can coral be soft and hard? What likes to hide in coral? Where might some fish find their food?*
pages 10–11: Ask, *What type of animals are sharks? Where do they live? What type of teeth do they have? Do sharks have very strong jaws? What do sharks eat? Are sharks good at smelling/seeing/hearing? Do you think sharks can hear fish that are far away?*
pages 12–13: Ask, *What are the biggest animals in the ocean? Are whales fish? What do whales breathe? What is their blowhole for? What do whales eat? How do whales swim? What do they use their tail and fins for?*
pages 14–15: Ask, *What is the underwater world full of? What might you see if you were snorkelling and looked down into the beautiful world? What animals and plants are part of the ocean? Why do we need to know about the animals and plants in the ocean?*
page 16: Ask, *Where did we see these words in the text? What do these words mean?* Discuss that the glossary shows us the meaning of words that are in the text. Read through the words and talk about what they mean.

Reading the text

- Have children read independently. Focus on meaning, structure and visual cues. Support development of reading strategies. Identify areas that challenge children and can be developed into future learning experiences.
- Ask children to relate the text to their own experiences. Ask, *What underwater animal/plants have you seen? Where have you seen underwater animals or plants?*
- Have children retell the text in their own words.
- Discuss how the purpose of this text is to teach readers about plants and animals that live in the underwater world. Ask, *What did you learn from reading this text?*
- Ask inferential questions such as: *Why do we need to take care of the ocean? Why might sharks need to smell? What might the coral protect the fish from? If whales use their blowhole for breathing, what do they use their mouth for?*

After reading

Focus on meaning, structure and visual cues that children found difficult while reading. Discuss strategies and provide opportunities for children to consolidate specific skills. For example, if children had difficulty with the word 'colourful', discuss strategies such as sounding out the phonemes, re-reading, looking at the pictures or using the sentence content.

Choose from the following activities.

Comprehension

- *True or false:* Have children recall facts that they learnt from reading the text. Write some true and false sentences about the text on the board and discuss
- why they are true or false. Have children complete **PW 46** (page 78), identifying if the sentences are true or false.
- *Compare and contrast:* Ask children to write facts about turtles and fish on pieces of paper. Place two overlapping hoops on the ground and explain how a Venn diagram works. As a group, have children sort and place their facts on turtles and fish into the appropriate hoops. Have children complete **PW 47** (page 79), sorting facts in a Venn diagram.

Phonological awareness

- Find 'lay' in the text and discuss the vowel digraph 'ay'. Model the sound these letters make when they are together. Brainstorm and record other 'ay' words. Repeat for 'ee' in 'need', 'ea' in 'sea' and 'aw' in 'jaws'.
- Find 'hard' in the text. Discuss the sound made when the letters 'ar' are together. Talk about how 'hard' can be read by sounding 'h-ar-d'. Find and record other 'ar' words in the text (e.g. 'shark', 'sharp').
- Find 'bright' in the text and model how it can be sounded as 'br-igh-t'. Discuss the sound the letters 'igh' make. Brainstorm and list other 'igh' words.
- Find the antonyms 'soft' and 'hard' in the text. Explain that antonyms are words that mean the opposite. Ask children to find something in the room that is soft and something in the room that is hard. Encourage them to explain the difference between 'soft' and 'hard'. Repeat for 'big' and 'small'. Brainstorm and record other antonyms.
- Talk about split vowel digraphs and how the first vowel is a long vowel. Find 'made' and 'like' in the text and have children practise sounding them. Ask them to find other words in the text that have split vowel digraphs.
- Discuss the consonant digraph 'th'. Talk about how these letters are sounded together to make one sound. Discuss how 'th' can be at the beginning, middle or end of words.
- Talk about the word 'shell' and the consonant digraph 'sh'. Discuss the sound these letters make together. Ask children to find 'sh' words in the text.

Vocabulary

- *Visual recognition of high-frequency words:* 'beautiful', 'because', 'carefully', 'colourful', 'know', 'smaller', 'smallest', 'such'. Ask children to find these words in the text. Write the words on cards (two cards for each word) and play games, such as Concentration and Snap.
- *Theme words—underwater:* Write nouns from the text on a piece of paper. Next to each word, have children draw a picture to show its meaning. As a group, think of a simple definition for each word and record it next to the word and the picture. Have children complete **PW 48** (page 80), drawing pictures of words and writing sentences to explain their meanings.

Fluency

- Discuss the importance of reading smoothly and without stopping. Demonstrate how to read fluently. Have children practise by reading the text to each other.

Text conventions

- *Features of the front cover:* Look at the front cover and ask children to identify the title and author. Explain to children that the author wrote the text.
- *Features of the back cover:* As a group, look at the back cover and have children identify the blurb. Discuss how readers can read the blurb to get an idea of what the text will be about. Ask, *Does the blurb match what the text was about?*

Writing

- Discuss how this text teaches readers lots of information about animals and plants that live in the underwater world. Ask children to write a report about their favourite underwater animal, including what it looks like, where it lives, what it does and what it eats. Have children draw and label a diagram of the animal.

▶ ELL engagement

- Collect pictures of animals and plants that live under the sea. Discuss these with children and as a group make a list of them. Provide children with large pieces of paper, paint, glue, card, boxes, material and other craft materials. Have children make an underwater world mural, painting the paper blue and using the other craft materials to make underwater animals and plants to paste onto their mural. During the activity, focus on enhancing and supporting children's language and communication skills.

▶ Assessment

- PWs 46, 47 and 48 completed
- Note the child's responses, attempts and reading behaviours before, during and after reading
- Collect work samples, e.g. PW 46 could be kept in the child's portfolio
- Complete Running Record (page 136)

Name: ______________________ Date: ______________

True or false

- Read the facts about the text.
- Circle *True* if the facts are correct. Circle *False* if the facts are wrong.

Under the sea is a beautiful world full of plants and animals.	*True*	*False*
Fish can be big and they can be small.	*True*	*False*
Turtles don't live under water all the time.	*True*	*False*
You can see seaweed and seagrass under the sea.	*True*	*False*
All coral is very hard.	*True*	*False*
Small fish like to hide in the coral because it is a safe place.	*True*	*False*
Sharks are big fish that live in the ocean.	*True*	*False*
Sharks don't eat meat because they only eat plants.	*True*	*False*
Whales are the smallest animals in the ocean.	*True*	*False*
Whales are big fish.	*True*	*False*
Whales swim by moving their tails up and down.	*True*	*False*
If you snorkel you can see the beautiful world under the sea.	*True*	*False*
We need to take care of the animals and plants in the ocean.	*True*	*False*

Main teaching focus
Comprehension: Answering true or false questions.

Other teaching focus
Comprehension: Recalling information from the text.

Teacher's note
Children read the sentences, decide if the facts are correct or wrong and circle True or False.

Engage Literacy is published in 2013 by Raintree • *Underwater World*, Level 18. This page may be photocopied for educational use within the purchasing institution.

Name: ______________________ Date: ______________

Compare and contrast

- Write facts that are only about sharks in the left circle.
- Write facts that are only about whales in the right circle.
- Write facts that are about both sharks and whales in the middle.

Refer to pages 10–13 in the book to help you.

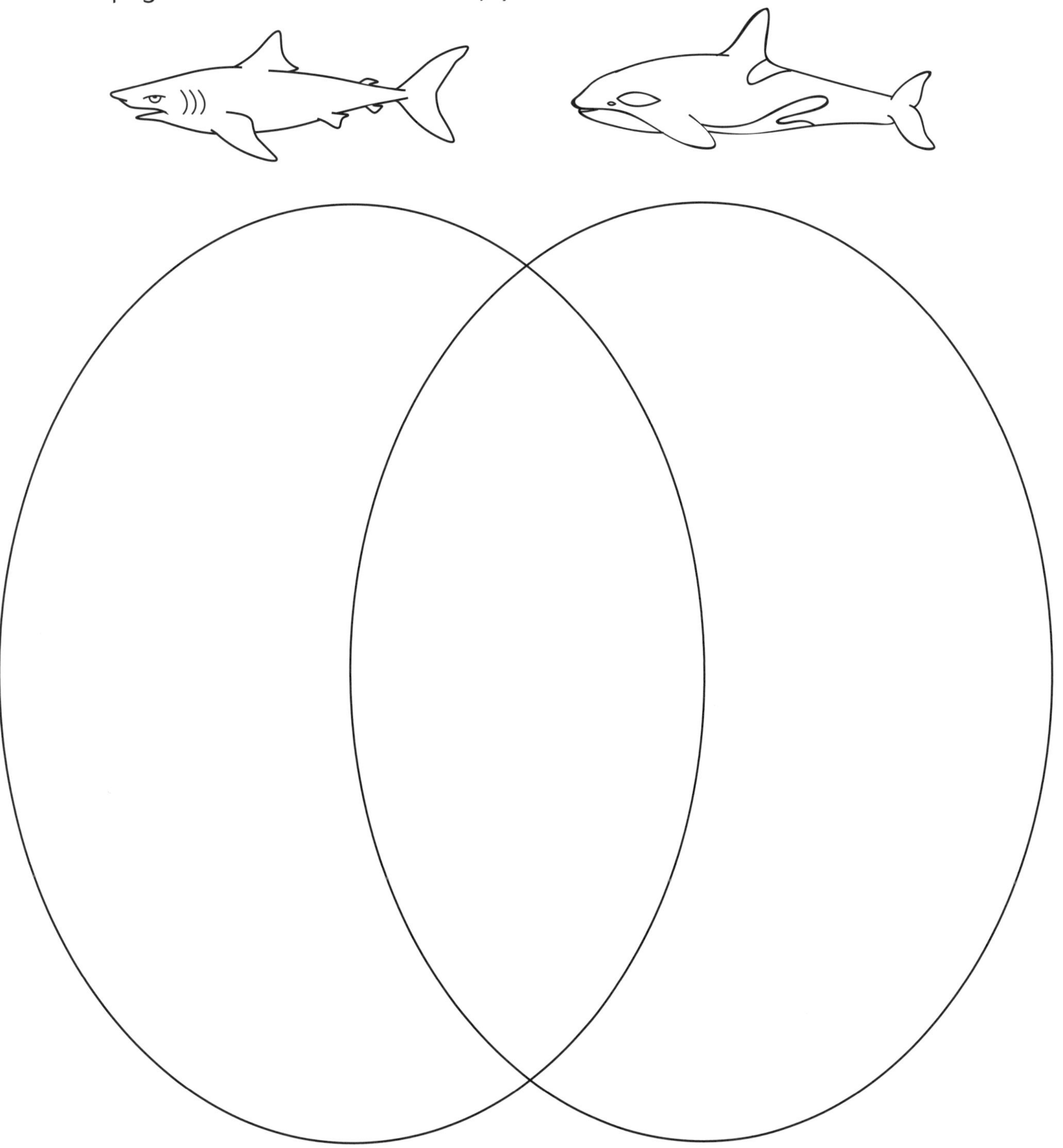

Main teaching focus
Comprehension: Comparing and contrasting.

Other teaching focus
Comprehension: Recalling information from the text.

Teacher's note
Children record facts about sharks in the left circle, facts about whales in the right circle and facts that are true for both in the middle.

Engage Literacy is published in 2013 by Raintree • *Underwater World*, Level 18. This page may be photocopied for educational use within the purchasing institution.

PW 48

Name: ______________________ Date: ______________

Word meanings

You will need: coloured pencils

- Draw a picture to match each word.
- Write a sentence explaining the meaning of the word.

Word	Picture	Meaning
starfish		
shark		
blowhole		
jaws		
coral		
seaweed		
whale		
turtle		
fish		

Main teaching focus
Vocabulary: Word meanings.

Other teaching focus
Comprehension: Finding word meanings using context of sentence.

Teacher's note
Children draw a picture to show the meaning of the words. Then they write a definition for each word.

Engage Literacy is published in 2013 by Raintree • *Underwater World*, Level 18. This page may be photocopied for educational use within the purchasing institution.

Holly's Three White Mice

Level 19 **Fiction** **Word count:** 485 **Text type:** Narrative

HFW introduced: arrived, covered, follow, followed, idea, quietly, terrible, through, whispered

HFW consolidated: easy, even, glad, I've, might, sadly, special

Linking text: *Mouse Visor* (non-fiction)

Curriculum link: me/family, animals/pets, community

Phonic awareness: vowel digraphs 'ay', 'ou', 'or'; 'c' making 's' phoneme; suffixes 'ed', 'ly'; initial consonant digraph 'qu'; rhyming words with 'ight' and 'ite' endings; root word 'all'; 'y' making long vowel sound 'ee'

Story summary: When Holly's family go on a fishing trip, her three white mice escape from their box. The kitchen is a big mess, but Holly follows the tiny white footprints and finds her mice in the doll's house.

Tuning in

- Talk about mice. Have children describe what they look like, how they move and what they like to eat. Encourage children to role-play the movements of mice.

Book walk

- Introduce the story. Give each child a copy of the book and discuss the title. Ask children to share what they think the story will be about. Have children make predictions, using the title and cover illustration as prompts. Ask, *Who do you think Holly is? Why does she have three white mice? What might happen to the mice?*
- Flip through the book, discussing events and illustrations. Promote language that is used throughout the text. Discuss how illustrations help us to read the text. When questioning, use vocabulary from the text.

pages 2–3: Ask, *What animal does Holly love? What colour mice does she love? Which mice does she love most of all? Where do her three pet white mice live?*
pages 4–5: Ask, *Do you think Holly wants to go on the overnight fishing trip with her family or does she want to stay home with her three mice? Who will take care of Holly's mice? Should Mrs Brooks come and feed the mice in the afternoon? What might Holly tell her mice before she goes?*
pages 6–7: Ask, *What are the mice running up? What are they pushing their way through? Do you think the mice had a lovely time running all over the house? Where do you think they ran in the house? What would they have been looking for when they ran into the kitchen? What would Mrs Brooks have found in the box that afternoon? Is she upset? Where is she looking for the mice? Has she found them anywhere?*
pages 8–9: Ask, *What would Mrs Brooks be telling Holly now that she has arrived home? What is running down Holly's cheek?*
pages 10–11: Ask, *What did they see when they walked into the kitchen? Where is the terrible mess? What is covering the bench and the floor? Who might have made the flour go everywhere? What has Holly picked up? What is in the corner of the box?*
pages 12–13: Ask, *Where have the naughty mice been? Why do they need to find the mice quickly? What footprints can they see going down the hall? Why are they following the footprints?*
pages 14–15: Ask, *What footprints do they follow? Where do the footprints go? What goes through the door of the doll's house, up the stairs and into the bedroom? Why is Holly down on her knees and peeking through the window?*
page 16: Ask, *Where are the naughty white mice fast asleep? Would Holly be glad to see the mice even though they are very naughty? Who just opened their eyes and blinked?*

Reading the text

- Have children read independently. Focus on meaning, structure and visual cues. Support development of reading strategies. Identify areas that challenge children and can be developed into future learning experiences.
- Ask children to relate the text to their own experiences. Ask, *Have you had a pet that has run away? Did you find your missing pet?*
- Have children retell the story in their own words and discuss what happened in the beginning, middle and end.
- Ask inferential questions such as: *What could Holly have done to keep her mice safe inside their box? Why couldn't Mrs Brooks find Holly's three white mice? Why do you think the mice wanted to get out of their box? Why is there a tear running down Holly's cheek? Who put the hole in the box of flour? Who do you think should clean up the mess in the kitchen?*

After reading

Focus on meaning, structure and visual cues that children found difficult while reading. Discuss strategies and provide opportunities for children to consolidate specific skills. For example, if children had difficulty with the word 'naughty', discuss strategies such as sounding out the phonemes, re-reading, looking at the illustrations or using the sentence content.

Choose from the following activities.

Comprehension

- *Characters:* Have children recall the characters—Holly, Mum, Dad, Mrs Brooks and the three mice. Discuss their role in the story. Draw a picture of each character on a separate piece of paper. Ask children to write sentences about each character on the paper, e.g. descriptions, feelings, actions. Encourage children to compare and contrast the characters by explaining how they were the same or different. Have children use **PW 49** (page 83) to make a mobile showing the characters, their feelings and actions.
- *Sequencing—time order words:* Flip through the text and have children discuss the events. Ask, *What happened in the beginning/middle/end?* Write 'first', 'then', 'next', 'after', 'later' and 'finally' on flash cards. Have children each draw a different event from the text. As a group, have children sequence their pictures in the correct order and place the time order word flash cards next to the appropriate picture. Have children complete **PW 50** (page 84), sequencing pictures and matching them to time order words.

Phonological awareness

- Discuss the word 'stay'. Talk about the vowel digraph 'ay' and model the sound these letters make together. Have children find other 'ay' words in the text. Ask them to think of other 'ay' words. Repeat for 'ou' and 'mouse'.
- Talk about how the letter 'c' in 'mice' makes the sound of the letter 's'. Ask, *Can you think of any other words where the letter 'c' makes the sound of the letter 's', e.g., 'city', 'advice'?*
- Talk about how the suffix 'ed' can be added to the end of words. Have children find words in the text that end with 'ed' and practise reading them. Talk about how if there is an 'ed' on the end of a word it means it has already happened (i.e. past tense). Repeat for the 'ly' suffix in 'quietly'. Discuss how the 'ly' suffix means the word is telling us how something is being done.
- Talk about the initial consonant digraph 'qu' making the sound 'cw' at the beginning of 'quietly'. Model the sound that the letters 'q' and 'u' make together. Brainstorm and list other words that begin with 'qu' and have children circle the 'qu' digraphs.
- Find 'corner' in the text. Discuss the sound made when the letters 'or' are together. Brainstorm and record 'or' words and have children practise sounding them.
- As a group, talk about how 'white' and 'might' rhyme because their ending sounds the same. Talk about how words can rhyme even though they have different letter patterns at the end. Ask, *Can you think of any other words that rhyme with 'might' and 'white'?* (e.g. 'kite', 'sight', 'fight') Record these words and ask children to identify the 'ight' or 'ite' ending of them.
- Find 'all' in the text. Talk about how new words can be made by adding letters to the start of this word. Have children find 'small'. Ask, *Can you see the word 'all' in this word?* Cover up the 'sm' and have children find 'all'. Ask, *What other words could we make by putting letters in front of the word 'all'?* (e.g. 'tall', 'hall', 'fall', 'call') Record these and have children underline 'all' in each word.
- Find 'Holly' in the text. Discuss how the 'y' ending makes the long vowel 'ee' sound. Have children find other words in the text with a 'y' ending that makes this sound, e.g. 'sleepy', 'sorry'. Encourage children to practise reading and sounding these words.

Vocabulary

- *Visual recognition of high-frequency words:* 'arrived', 'covered', 'follow', 'followed', 'idea', 'quietly', 'terrible', 'through', 'whispered'. Have children find these words in the text. Give the children blank flash cards, have them write a high-frequency word on each card and arrange the cards in alphabetical order.

Fluency

- Discuss the importance of reading smoothly and without stopping. Demonstrate how to read fluently. Have children practise by reading the text to each other.

Text conventions

- *Exclamation marks:* Talk about how exclamation marks are used to show that something is important or exciting and they influence the way the text is read. Ask children to practise reading the sentences with exclamation marks and compare how they would be read without exclamation marks.
- *Speech marks:* Explain that text between speech marks is what a character is saying. Turn to page 12 and have children role-play the conversation between Holly and Mum. Repeat with other pages from the text.

Writing

- Have children draw a map of Holly's house, including the kitchen, hall, stairs and Holly's bedroom. Ask children to draw the mice's footprints to show where the mice went after they escaped. Ask children to write sentences explaining where the mice went. Encourage them to use time order words (i.e. 'first', 'then', 'next', 'after', 'later', 'finally') at the beginning of sentences.

▸ ELL engagement

- Show children pictures of mice and ask them to describe and share what they know about mice. Draw a large picture of a mouse on a piece of paper and have children label the different parts of its body. Have children use **PW 51** (page 85) to make a mouse, then retell how they made it.

▸ Assessment

- PWs 49, 50 and 51 completed
- Note the child's responses, attempts and reading behaviours before, during and after reading
- Collect work samples, e.g. PW 49 could be kept in the child's portfolio
- Complete Running Record (page 137)

Name: ______________________________ Date: _____________

Character mobile

You will need: coloured pencils, scissors, five pieces of string, tape, coat hanger or stick

- Colour and cut round the characters.
- Write about each character on the back of the pictures.
- Tape string onto the top of each picture.
- Tape the other end of the string onto a coat hanger or stick.

Main teaching focus
Comprehension: Recalling and discussing characters; inferring characters' feelings.

Other teaching focus
Comprehension: Comparing and contrasting characters.

Teacher's note
Children colour and cut round the pictures. They write a description of the characters on the back. They tape string to the top of each picture and attach the other end of the string to the coat hanger or stick.

Engage Literacy is published in 2013 by Raintree • *Holly's Three White Mice*, Level 19. This page may be photocopied for educational use within the purchasing institution.

PW 50

Name: ______________________ Date: ____________

Sequencing

You will need: coloured pencils, scissors, glue, a piece of paper

- Colour and cut out the pictures. Paste them in the correct order in the boxes.
- Write matching sentences for each picture on another piece of paper. You can refer to the story to help you.

1 First ...	2 Then ...	3 Next ...

4 After ...	5 Later ...	6 Finally ...

Main teaching focus
Comprehension: Sequencing events from the text; time order words.

Other teaching focus
Comprehension: Recalling events from the text.

Teacher's note
Children colour and cut out the pictures. They sequence the pictures and paste them in the correct order in the boxes. Children then write what happened in the story on another piece of paper.

Engage Literacy is published in 2013 by Raintree • *Holly's Three White Mice*, Level 19. This page may be photocopied for educational use within the purchasing institution.

Name: ______________________ Date: ____________

Make a mouse

You will need: coloured pencils, scissors, glue, cotton wool, cotton thread

- Colour the parts of the mouse.
- Cut them out and paste them together.
- Paste some cotton wool onto your mouse to make fur.
- Add some cotton thread for the whiskers.

Main teaching focus	**Other teaching focus**	**Teacher's note**
Oral language development: Language and vocabulary development.	*Oral language development:* Retelling an experience.	Children colour and cut out the parts of the mouse. Then they paste them together and stick cotton wool onto the mouse as the fur and cotton thread as the whiskers. Children retell how they made their mouse.

Engage Literacy is published in 2013 by Raintree • *Holly's Three White Mice*, Level 19. This page may be photocopied for educational use within the purchasing institution.

Go-Kart Surprise

Level 19 **Fiction** **Word count:** 467 **Text type:** Narrative

HFW introduced: arrived, knew, really, sped, yelled

HFW consolidated: almost, sadly, thought, wasn't, watch, watched

Linking text: *A Go-Kart at School* (non-fiction)

Curriculum link: me/family, community, physically active

Phonic awareness: vowel digraphs 'oo', 'ar', 'er'; 'c' making 's' phoneme; consonant digraph 'ph'; 'ould' letter string; contractions 'wasn't', 'didn't', 'you're'; three-letter consonant phonemes 'str'

Story summary: Justin wants to race in a go-kart and thinks it's unfair that his brother Mick gets to have all the fun. Then Mum takes him to the go-kart track and Justin has his first go-kart race!

Tuning in

- Talk about go-karts. Ask, *What is a go-kart? Have you been in a go-kart before?* Have children pretend to drive a go-kart. Make a 'go-kart track' around the classroom and have children participate in a 'go-kart race'. Discuss the noise go-karts make and how fast go-karts go.
- Talk about surprises. Ask, *What is a surprise? Have you been surprised before?* Discuss things that people do to surprise others. Have children show a surprised expression on their faces. Ask, *Do surprises make people happy or sad?*

Book walk

- Introduce the story. Give each child a copy of the book and discuss the title. Ask children to share what they think the story will be about. Have children make predictions, using the title and cover illustration as prompts. Ask children to think of words that might be in the text.
- Flip through the book, discussing events and illustrations. Promote language that is used throughout the text. Discuss how illustrations help us to read the text. When questioning, use vocabulary from the text.

pages 2–3: Ask, *Is Justin able to race or is he too little? Who gave Mick his crash helmet and gloves? Do you think Justin might be able to race next week when it's his eighth birthday? Did Mick put on his helmet and gloves? Who jumped into the go-kart and zoomed off for a practice lap?*
pages 4–5: Ask, *Who does Justin think gets to have all the fun? Does Justin get to race or does he just watch and help out? Why do you think Justin doesn't say anything?*
pages 6–7: Ask, *What does Justin want to do? When will Justin get to race? Has the race started? What is zooming past?*
pages 8–9: Ask, *What does Justin watch speed around the track? What colour go-kart does Mick overtake around the last corner? Who wins the race? What is Justin thinking? Does Justin think he would be a great go-kart driver?*
pages 10–11: Ask, *What are they having for dinner? Who is happy? Would Mum think that it was a great race? Is Justin hungry? Where is Mick's trophy? How do you think Justin is feeling?*
pages 12–13: Ask, *Whose birthday is it the next Saturday? How many friends come to his party? What are they eating? Does Justin look like he is having fun? What has Mum come out with? Where might they be going to in the van?*
pages 14–15: Ask, *Where has Mum taken them? Is Mick at the track with some of his friends? How many go-karts are there waiting on the track? Why is Justin excited? What do they need to put on first?*
page 16: Ask, *Are they ready to race once everyone has their safety gear on and they have gone over the rules? What number is on Justin's go-kart? Is it race time for Justin now?*

Reading the text

- Have children read independently. Focus on meaning, structure and visual cues. Support development of reading strategies. Identify areas that challenge children and can be developed into future learning experiences.
- Ask children to relate the text to their own experiences. Ask, *Is there anything that you have had to wait till you were older to do? What things have you been upset or jealous about?*
- Have children retell the story in their own words and discuss what happened in the beginning, middle and end.
- Talk about the characters, setting and plot of the text.
- Discuss that this is a narrative text and talk about the features of narrative text.
- Ask inferential questions such as: *Why do you think Justin had to wait until he was eight before he could start go-karting? Why wasn't Justin hungry at dinner? Why wasn't Justin having fun at his party?*

After reading

Focus on meaning, structure and visual cues that children found difficult while reading. Discuss strategies and provide opportunities for children to consolidate specific skills. For example, if children had difficulty with the word 'ready', discuss strategies such as sounding out the phonemes, re-reading,

looking at the illustrations or using the sentence content.
Choose from the following activities.

Comprehension

- *Crossword:* Have children discuss the story. Ask comprehension questions, for example: *What did Justin want to do? How many friends came to his party? Did Mick win his race? How old was Justin when he was allowed to race?* If children are unsure of the answers, encourage them to re-read the text. Discuss how to do crosswords. Explain the difference between 'across' words and 'down' words. Have children complete the crossword on **PW 52** (page 88).
- *Characters, setting, plot:* As a group, recall and draw the characters on the board. Ask children to talk about and draw the setting on the board. Ask children to retell the plot. As a group, write a summary of the main events on the board. Have children complete **PW 53** (page 89), writing a book report about the text.

Phonological awareness

- Find 'zoomed' in the text and discuss the vowel digraph 'oo'. Model how these letters make a long sound in this word. Ask children to brainstorm other words that contain this sound.
- Find 'start' in the text. Discuss the sound made when the letters 'ar' are together. Talk about how 'start' can be read by sounding 's-t-ar-t'. Have children identify other 'ar' words in the text and practise reading them. Brainstorm and record other 'ar' words.
- As a group, talk about 'er' at the end of 'brother'. Model the sound these letters make together. Ask, *Can you think of any other words that have the 'er' sound?*
- Discuss how the 'c' in 'race' makes the sound of the letter 's'. Ask, *Can you think of any other words where the 'c' makes the sound of the letter 's'?* Find 'place' in the text and have children sound the letter 'c' in this word.
- Talk about the consonant digraph 'ph' in 'trophy'. Explain how these letters are not sounded separately as 'p-h' but are sounded together. Model the sound these letters make. Ask, *When we sound these letters together, what letter sound does it sound like?*
- Have children find 'could' in the text. Talk about the 'ould' letter string and the sound these letters make when they are together. Ask, *Can you think of any other words that end with 'ould'?* Record these words, have children circle the 'ould' ending and then ask children to practise sounding them.
- Talk about the contraction 'wasn't'. Write 'was not' and 'wasn't' on the board and discuss how the contraction has an apostrophe instead of the letter 'o'. Repeat for 'didn't' and 'you're'. Find the contractions in the text.
- Ask children to find 'stripes' in the text. Discuss the three-letter phonemes 'str' at the beginning. Explain how these letters are sounded as 'str' to make one sound, rather than sounded separately as 's-t-r'. Ask, *Can you think of other words that begin with 'str'?*

Vocabulary

- *Visual recognition of high-frequency words:* 'arrived', 'knew', 'really', 'sped', 'yelled'. Ask children to find these words in the text. Write the words on cards (two cards for each word) and play games, such as Concentration and Snap.
- Have children spell the high-frequency words by moulding the letters with play dough.

Fluency

- Discuss the importance of reading smoothly and without stopping. Demonstrate how to read fluently. Have children practise by reading the text to each other.

Text conventions

- *Features of the front cover:* Look at the front cover of the text and ask children to identify the title, author and illustrator. Explain to children that the author is the person who wrote the text and the illustrator is the person who drew the pictures. Ask, *What is the title of the text? Who is the author? Who is the illustrator?*
- *Features of the back cover:* As a group, look at the back cover and have children identify the blurb. Discuss how readers can read the blurb to get an idea of what the text will be about. Ask, *Does the blurb match what the text is about?*

Writing

- Have children write an acrostic poem about go-karts, writing words, sentences or phrases about go-karts that begin with each of the letters in the word.

▶ ELL engagement

- As a group, brainstorm what you might see at a go-kart track. Use the illustrations in the text as a prompt. Encourage children to label and describe things that they see in the illustrations to enhance their vocabulary development. Make a list of 'go-kart' words. Enlarge a copy of **PW 54** (page 90) on A3 paper for each child and have them make their own go-kart track and go-karts. When they have completed this, encourage children to play with their tracks and go-karts together. During this time, support children in communicating and working together. Have children retell how they made their go-karts and track.

▶ Assessment

- PWs 52, 53 and 54 completed
- Note the child's responses, attempts and reading behaviours before, during and after reading
- Collect work samples, e.g. PW 52 could be kept in the child's portfolio
- Complete Running Record (page 138)

PW 52

Name: ______________________ Date: ____________

Crossword

- Write the answers to the questions in the crossword puzzle.

Across

3 Justin wants to race in a go-________.

4 Where did Mick come in the race?

6 How many friends were at Justin's party?

9 The title of the book is 'Go-Kart ________.'

10 How old did Justin turn?

Down

1 Justin was too ________ to race.

2 What did they eat at the party?

5 The race was at the go-kart ________.

7 Who took Justin to the track?

8 What did Mick win?

Main teaching focus
Comprehension: Answering questions about a text; recalling information from a text.

Other teaching focus
Writing: Spelling.

Teacher's note
Children answer the 'across' and 'down' questions. They write the answers in the crossword puzzle.

Engage Literacy is published in 2013 by Raintree • *Go-Kart Surprise*, Level 19. This page may be photocopied for educational use within the purchasing institution.

Name: ______________________________ Date: ______________

Book report

You will need: coloured pencils

- Write the title, author and illustrator of the text.
- Write and draw about the characters, setting and your favourite part of the plot.

Title
Author
Illustrator
Characters
Setting
Plot

Main teaching focus
Comprehension: Recalling the characters, setting and plot of a text.

Other teaching focus
Text conventions: Front cover of a text—identifying title, author and illustrator.

Teacher's note
Children fill in the boxes by writing the title, author and illustrator of the text. Then they write and draw about the characters, setting and their favourite part of the plot.

Engage Literacy is published in 2013 by Raintree • *Go-Kart Surprise*, Level 19. This page may be photocopied for educational use within the purchasing institution.

Name: ______________________________ Date: ______________

Go-kart track

You will need: coloured pencils, scissors

- Colour the go-kart track and the go-karts.
- Cut them out and play with them!

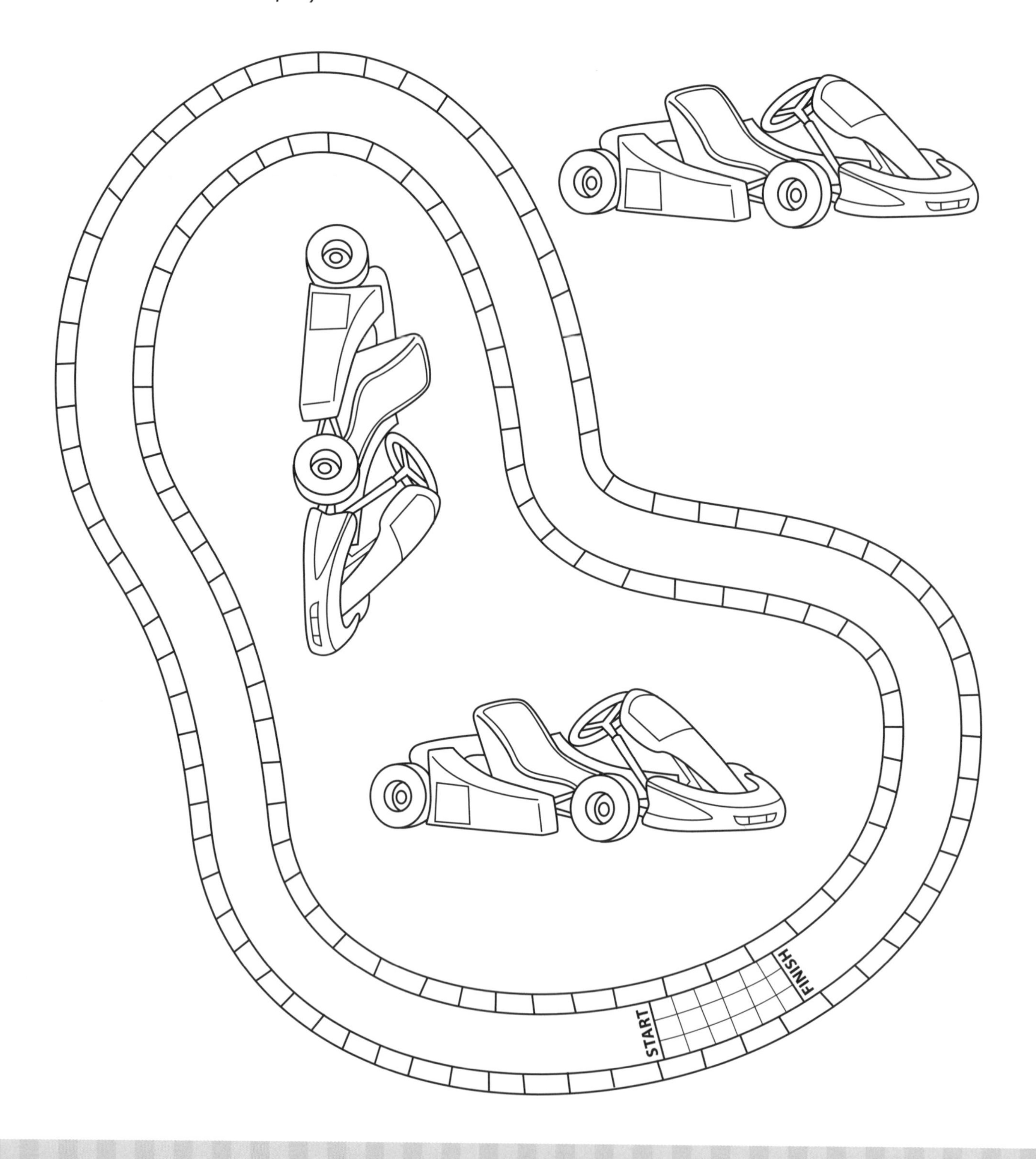

Main teaching focus
Oral language: Developing language and vocabulary.

Other teaching focus
Oral language: Retelling an experience; communicating.

Teacher's note
Enlarge a copy of the PW on A3 paper for each child. Children colour the go-kart track and the go-karts. Then they cut them out and have a go-kart race!

Engage Literacy is published in 2013 by Raintree • *Go-Kart Surprise*, Level 19. This page may be photocopied for educational use within the purchasing institution.

Mouse Visor

Level 19 **Non-fiction** **Word count:** 403 **Text type:** Procedural

HFW introduced: doesn't, instead, together, wear
HFW consolidated: because, between, carefully, easy, favourite, might
Linking text: *Holly's Three White Mice* (fiction)
Curriculum link: creative play, animals
Phonic awareness: vowel digraphs 'ou', 'ea', 'ey', 'ee', 'or'; contraction 'doesn't'; split vowel digraphs 'a_e', 'o_e'; syllables
Text summary: Learn how to make a mouse visor to wear on your head.

Tuning in

- Ask, *Who wears hats? Can anyone think of any different hats? What is a visor?* Show children a visor. Ask, *How are they the same? How are they different?*

Book walk

- Introduce the text. Give each child a copy of the book and discuss the title. Ask children to share what they think the text will be about.
- Have children read the blurb on the back cover. Ask, *Now that you have read the blurb, what do you think the text will be about? How did the blurb help you make your prediction?*
- Flip through the book, discussing events and photographs. Promote language that is used throughout the text. Discuss how photographs help us to read the text. When questioning, use vocabulary from the text.

pages 2–3: Ask, *Do you think it is hard to make a mouse visor? Could you wear it as soon as you have made it? What is a visor like? What will you need to make your mouse visor?*
pages 4–5: Ask, *Why might you make the face and ears first? What is the boy cutting out to make the mouse's face? What shape is he cutting out of the grey card? Would it need to be a big shape so it fits around your head? Which part do you think will be the mouse's face?*
pages 6–7: Ask, *How many circles do you cut out from the grey card? What will these two circles be? How many small circles do you cut out from the pink card? Where do you paste the pink circles? What have they made? Where do you paste the ears?*
pages 8–9: Ask, *How do you think you would make the nose and cheeks of the mouse? How many big brown pompoms do you paste onto your mouse's face? What would the brown pompoms be on the mouse? What colour pompom do you paste between the two brown pompoms? Is the pink pompom smaller or bigger than the brown pompoms? What would the pink pompom be?*
pages 10–11: Ask, *How many googly eyes would you need to paste on? Where would be a good place to paste the eyes? How do you cut the three pipe cleaners? Who might you need to ask for some help? Where do you paste the pipe cleaners? What do the pipe cleaners look like? What could you use instead of pipe cleaners?*
pages 12–13: Ask, *How would you see if your visor fits your head? What do you put the visor around? How do you work out where the ends meet? What will the teacher need to do when you take the visor off your head? Could your teacher use staples or tape?*
pages 14–15: Ask, *Is the mouse visor ready to wear? Could you make more mice? How are these mice different?*
page 16: Ask, *What do these words mean?* Discuss that the glossary shows us the meaning of words that are in the text. Read through the words and talk about what they mean.

Reading the text

- Have children read independently. Focus on meaning, structure and visual cues. Support development of reading strategies. Identify areas that challenge children and can be developed into future learning experiences.
- Discuss that the purpose of this text is to teach readers how to make a mouse visor. Ask, *Could you make a mouse visor after reading this text? What things does this text explain to you? What do we learn how to make when we read this?*
- Talk about how this is a non-fiction procedural text.
- Ask inferential questions such as: *How would you use the wool or string to make the whiskers? Why do the pipe cleaners need to be cut in half? Why would you need strong paste to stick the whiskers on? How might you make a visor that looks like a different animal?*

After reading

Focus on meaning, structure and visual cues that children found difficult while reading. Discuss strategies and provide opportunities for children to consolidate specific skills. For example, if children had difficulty with the word 'shape', discuss strategies such as sounding out the phonemes, re-reading, looking at the pictures or using the sentence content.

Choose from the following activities.

Comprehension

- *Sequence sentences:* As a group, flip through the text and have children talk about the steps involved in making the mouse visor. Copy sentences from the text onto strips of paper. Give the strips of paper to the children and

have them read and then sequence them in the correct order. As a group, read through the steps to ensure that they make sense. Have children complete **PW 55** (page 93), sequencing sentences.
- *Recall:* Collect the materials needed to make the mouse visor. Hold up each item and ask children how this will be used. Have children complete **PW 56** (page 94), recalling how items are used to make a mouse visor.

Phonological awareness

- Find 'mouse' in the text and talk about the vowel digraph 'ou'. Model to children the sound that these letters make together. Have children find 'ou' words in the text.
- Talk about the 'ea' vowel digraph in 'ears'. Discuss the long sound 'ea' makes in this word. Then talk about the short sound 'ea' makes in 'head'. Ask children to find 'ea' words in the text and determine if they have a long or short sound.
- Find 'grey' in the text and discuss the vowel digraph 'ey'. Ask, *What sound do the letters 'ey' make in this word?* Ask children to find the word 'they' in the text. Have them identify and sound the 'ey' in this word.
- Find 'need' in the text. Discuss the vowel digraph 'ee' and model the sound that these letters make together. Brainstorm and record other 'ee' words and have children circle the 'ee' digraph in each word.
- Find 'visor' in the text. Discuss the sound made when the letters 'or' are together. Brainstorm and record other 'or' words and have children practise sounding them.
- Talk about the contraction 'doesn't'. Write 'does not' and 'doesn't' on the board and discuss how the contraction has an apostrophe instead of the letter 'o'. Have children find 'doesn't' in the text.
- Talk about split vowel digraphs and how the first vowel is a long vowel. Find 'make' and 'nose' in the text and have children practise sounding them. Ask them to find other words in the text that have split vowel digraphs.
- Discuss how many words have more than one syllable. Suggest some two and three syllable words and encourage the children to clap the syllables together, e.g., 'because', 'carefully', 'favourite'.

Vocabulary

- *Visual recognition of high-frequency words:* 'doesn't', 'instead', 'together', 'wear'. Ask children to find these words in the text. Have children write the words in three different writing styles.
- *Verbs:* As a group, talk about the verbs in the text. Explain how verbs are action words (words for actions that we can do). Find 'cut' in the text and ask children to role-play the action of cutting something. Ask children to find and list other verbs in the text.

Fluency

- Discuss the importance of reading smoothly and without stopping. Demonstrate how to read fluently. Have children practise by reading the text to each other.

Text conventions

- *Text emphasis/italic font:* Talk about how some words in the text are shown in italics. Discuss that this is because they are words that children might not recognise. Show children how these are the words in the glossary and we can find the meaning of the words by looking at the glossary on page 16.

Writing

- After making the mouse visor, have children write a recount about how they did it. Ensure children include the materials they needed and the steps they took to make the visor. Support children in sequencing their text into a beginning, middle and end. Encourage children to use time order words (i.e. 'first', 'then', 'next', 'after', 'later', 'finally') to sequence their ideas.

▸ ELL engagement

- Collect a variety of different hats or pictures of hats. Ask children to identify and name the different hats. Ask, *Who wears these different hats? Why do people wear these hats?* Discuss how hats are important because they protect us from the sun and cold. Talk about how some hats have a different purpose. Ask, *Why would someone wear a swimming cap?* Discuss how hats can be part of someone's uniform and how some hats are designed to protect our skull. Focus on building children's understanding and vocabulary during the discussion. Have children complete **PW 57** (page 95), identifying different hats and writing why they would be worn.

▸ Assessment

- PWs 55, 56 and 57 completed
- Note the child's responses, attempts and reading behaviours before, during and after reading
- Collect work samples, e.g. PW 55 could be kept in the child's portfolio
- Complete Running Record (page 139)

Name: ______________________ Date: ____________

Sequencing steps

You will need: scissors, glue, a piece of paper

- Cut out the sentences.
- Sort them in the right order and paste them onto the piece of paper.

Paste the ears onto the face of your mouse.

Paste on the small pink pompom. Paste it between the two brown pompoms. This is your mouse's nose.

Carefully cut three pipe cleaners in half. Paste the pipe cleaners each side of the brown pompoms so that they look like whiskers.

First, to make your mouse's face, cut out a big shape from the grey card.

The last thing you have to do is to see if your mouse visor fits. Take the visor off your head and ask your teacher to staple or tape it together.

Paste two big brown pompoms onto your mouse's face. These are your mouse's cheeks.

Now paste on the two googly eyes. These go just down from the ears.

Now cut out two circles from the grey card. Next, cut out two small circles from the pink card.

Main teaching focus
Comprehension: Sequencing sentences from the text.

Other teaching focus
Comprehension: Gaining meaning from text.

Teacher's note
Children cut out and read the sentences. Then they sort them in the correct sequence and paste them onto the piece of paper.

Engage Literacy is published in 2013 by Raintree • *Mouse Visor*, Level 19. This page may be photocopied for educational use within the purchasing institution.

Name: ______________________ Date: ____________

How do you make ...?

- Look at the pictures and fill in the table. Explain how you make the parts of the mouse visor.

	How do you make the mouse's face?	
	How do you make the ears?	
	How do you make the cheeks?	
	How do you make the nose?	
	How do you make the eyes?	
	How do you make the whiskers?	

Main teaching focus
Comprehension: Recalling events from the text; answering literal questions.

Other teaching focus
Writing: Writing instructions/a simple procedural text.

Teacher's note
Children look at the pictures and recall how the items are used to make the different parts of the mouse visor. Then they write the answers to the questions in the boxes.

Engage Literacy is published in 2013 by Raintree • *Mouse Visor*, Level 19. This page may be photocopied for educational use within the purchasing institution.

Name: ______________________________ Date: ______________

Hats

- Look at each hat.
- Write what type of hat it is and why people wear it.

	What type of hat is it?	Why do people wear this hat?

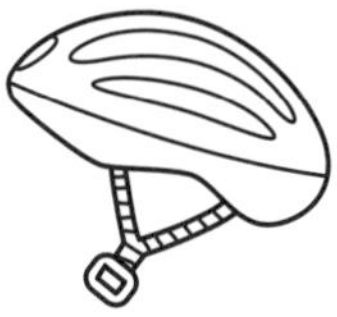		

Main teaching focus
Oral language: Developing language and vocabulary.

Other teaching focus
Oral language: Comparing and contrasting.

Teacher's note
Children look at the pictures of the hats. They write what type of hat it is and why someone would wear that hat.

Engage Literacy is published in 2013 by Raintree • *Mouse Visor*, Level 19. This page may be photocopied for educational use within the purchasing institution.

A Go-Kart at School

Level 19 **Non-fiction** **Word count:** 450 **Text type:** Exposition

HFW introduced: during, idea, important, learn, race, really, wear, weekend
HFW consolidated: easy, know, special, thought, watch
Linking text: *Go-Kart Surprise* (fiction)
Curriculum link: me/family, school, community, physically active
Phonic awareness: split vowel digraphs 'a_e', 'o_e', 'i_e'; vowel digraphs 'ee', 'ea', 'ow', 'oa', 'ar', 'ur'; rhyming words; consonant digraphs 'th', 'wh', 'ch'
Text summary: Read Clare's letter to her headteacher asking if she can bring her go-kart to school to show all the children. She has thought of lots of reasons why it would be a great idea.

Tuning in

- Have children bring something from home for show and tell. Ask each child to explain where they got it and what they do with it. Have children ask questions about each other's items. Discuss why it is good to have show and tell at school.

Book walk

- Introduce the text. Give each child a copy of the book and discuss the title. Ask children to share what they think the text will be about. Have children make predictions, using the title and cover pictures as prompts.
- Have children read the blurb on the back cover. Ask, *Now that you have read the blurb, what do you think the text will be about? How did the blurb help you make your prediction?*
- Flip through the book, discussing events and pictures. Promote language that is used throughout the text. Discuss how pictures help us to read the text. When questioning, use vocabulary from the text.

pages 2–3: Ask, *Who is the letter to? What does Clare Ling love to do? What does she do every weekend? Who goes go-kart racing with Clare? Who do think Clare wants to show her go-kart to?*
pages 4–5: Ask, *How old was Clare was when she started racing go-karts? Who do you think taught her? Do you think it would be hard to drive a go-kart? Do you think Clare wants the children in her class to have a ride in her go-kart? Would the mums and dads think it was a great idea?*
pages 6–7: Ask, *Who might bring the go-kart to school? Where would be the best place for the children to try out Clare's go-kart? Where is there a track that would be just right for a go-kart? Is the sports field close to the school buildings? Do go-karts make a lot of noise?*
pages 8–9: Ask, *What is important for people to wear when they are go-karting? What special clothes would they wear? How do the helmet and gloves keep Clare safe? Could Clare's dad bring special clothes, helmets and gloves for the other children? Who could help the children get into the special clothes so they are ready when it is their turn?*
pages 10–11: Ask, *What are some of the great things about racing go-karts? Would you learn about road rules? Would you learn about engines and how to steer? Would it be lots of fun? Would you make new friends?*
pages 12–13: Ask, *Is go-kart racing a great sport? Would it be fun for the children in Clare's class to learn something new? Do you think some children might go to Clare's go-karting club with her once they have had a turn?*
pages 14–15: Ask, *Who is the letter from? Do you think Clare wants Mr Ritter to like her idea?*
page 16: Ask, *Where did we see these words in the text? What do these words mean?* Discuss that the glossary shows us the meaning of words that are in the text. Read the words with the children and talk about what they mean.

Reading the text

- Have children read independently. Focus on meaning, structure and visual cues. Support development of reading strategies. Identify areas that challenge children and can be developed into future learning experiences.
- Have children retell in their own words what the text was about.
- Ask, *What is Clare trying to do by writing this letter? Why did she write the letter?*
- Ask inferential questions such as: *How would the helmet, gloves and special clothes help to keep the children safe? Do you think the other children would like the go-kart? Why/why not? Why is it lucky that the sports field is a long way from the buildings?*

After reading

Focus on meaning, structure and visual cues that children found difficult while reading. Discuss strategies and provide opportunities for children to consolidate specific skills. For example, if children had difficulty with the word 'racing', discuss strategies such as sounding out the phonemes,

re-reading, looking at the pictures or using the sentence content.

Choose from the following activities.

Comprehension

- *Writing questions:* Discuss what Clare wrote in her letter. Write the question stems 'who', 'what', 'when', 'where' and 'why' on the board. Discuss how these words can be used to form questions. Ask children to think of questions that begin with each of these words. Have children complete **PW 58** (page 98), writing questions to match sentences.
- *Summarising:* Talk about why Clare wrote the letter. Ask, *What were the main reasons that Clare gave for why she should bring her go-kart to school?* As a group, make a summary of the reasons Clare put in her letter. Have children complete **PW 59** (page 99), summarising the main ideas in the text.

Phonological awareness

- Talk about split vowel digraphs and how the first vowel is a long vowel. Find 'make', 'home' and 'drive' in the text and have children practise sounding them. Ask them to find other words in the text that have split vowel digraphs. Have children complete the activities on **PW 60** (page 100).
- As a group, find 'weekend' in the text. Discuss the vowel digraph 'ee' and model the sound that these letters make together. Brainstorm and record other 'ee' words and have children circle the 'ee' digraph in each word.
- Find 'really' in the text and discuss the vowel digraph 'ea'. Talk about the sound these letters make together. Discuss how the vowel digraph 'ea' in this word makes the same sound as the 'ee' in 'weekend'.
- Find 'know' in the text and talk about the 'ow' vowel digraph. Model the sound these letters make together. Brainstorm and record other 'ow' words. Repeat for 'oa' in 'road'. Discuss how these letters make the same sound as 'ow' in 'know'.
- Find 'start' in the text. Discuss the sound made when the letters 'ar' are together. Talk about how 'start' can be read by sounding 'st-ar-t'. Have children identify 'ar' words in the text and practise reading them. Brainstorm and record other 'ar' words.
- Find 'turn' in the text and talk about the sound made when the letters 'ur' are sounded together. Discuss how 'turn' can sounded as 't-ur-n'. Brainstorm and record other 'ur' words and have children identify 'ur' in each.
- Have children identify and read 'come' and 'some'. Discuss how these words rhyme because they sound the same at the end. Choose other words from the text and encourage children to think of rhyming words.
- Discuss the consonant phonemes 'th', 'wh' and 'ch'. Talk about the sound each digraph makes. Have children find 'th', 'wh' and 'ch' words in the text.

Vocabulary

- *Visual recognition of high-frequency words:* 'during', 'idea', 'important', 'learn', 'race', 'really', 'wear', 'weekend'. Ask children to find these words in the text. Write the words on cards (two cards for each word) and play games, such as Concentration and Snap.
- *Theme words—go-karts:* Brainstorm vocabulary related to go-karts, such as 'wheels', 'engine', 'race', 'seat', 'fast'. Record words on a piece of paper. Encourage children to use each word in a sentence to show their understanding of the word's meaning.

Fluency

- Discuss the importance of reading smoothly and without stopping. Demonstrate how to read fluently. Have children practise by reading the text to each other.

Text conventions

- *Text emphasis/italic font:* Talk about how some words in the text are shown in italics. Discuss that this is because they are words that children might not recognise. Show children that these words are in the glossary on page 16 and that we can find the meaning of the words by looking at the glossary.
- *Text type—letter:* Discuss how this text is a letter written from Clare to her headteacher. Help children to identify the features of the letter in the text.

Writing

- As a group, discuss what Mr Ritter might think when he reads the letter. Ask, *Do you think that Mr Ritter will let Clare bring her go-kart to school?* Discuss children's predictions. Ask children to write a letter to Clare, pretending that they are Mr Ritter. Ask them to explain in the letter whether or not Clare is allowed to bring her go-kart to school and give reasons why.

▶ ELL engagement

- Talk about go-kart races and have children describe what they would be like. Ask, *What other races can you think of?* Take children outside and have them participate in races using different sporting equipment. For example, have a bouncing ball race, a skipping race or a race where children need to balance a bean bag on their head. Discuss ordinal numbers (e.g. 'first', 'second', 'third') with children as they complete each race. Ask children to design other races using the equipment. During the activity, discuss the characteristics of someone who displays good sportsmanship.

▶ Assessment

- PWs 58, 59 and 60 completed
- Note the child's responses, attempts and reading behaviours before, during and after reading
- Collect work samples, e.g. PW 58 could be kept in the child's portfolio
- Complete Running Record (page 140)

Name: ______________________ Date: ____________

Writing questions

- Read the sentences.
- Write a question to match each sentence.

Go-kart racing is lots of fun and it is a great sport.

____

I started go-kart racing when I was eight years old.

____

When I race my go-kart, it is very important that I wear special clothes.

____

My dad can bring my go-kart to school any day.

____

I race my go-kart every weekend.

____

My dad is a really good teacher.

____

Main teaching focus
Comprehension: Writing a question to match a sentence; gaining meaning from text.

Other teaching focus
Text conventions: Question marks.

Teacher's note
Children read the sentences and then write questions on the lines underneath to match the sentences.

Engage Literacy is published in 2013 by Raintree • *A Go-Kart at School*, Level 19. This page may be photocopied for educational use within the purchasing institution.

Name: ______________________ Date: ______________

What did Clare think of?

- Write the main things Clare thought of when she wrote her letter.

1 ______________________________

____

2 ______________________________

____

3 ______________________________

____

4 ______________________________

____

5 ______________________________

____

6 ______________________________

____

Main teaching focus	Other teaching focus	Teacher's note
Comprehension: Summarising.	*Comprehension:* Recalling information from the text.	Children summarise the main ideas from the text and record the things that Clare thought about in the thought bubble.

Engage Literacy is published in 2013 by Raintree • *A Go-Kart at School*, Level 19. This page may be photocopied for educational use within the purchasing institution.

Name: ______________________ Date: ____________

PW 60

Split digraphs

You will need: coloured pencils

- Add 'e' at the end of each word to complete the split digraph. Draw a matching picture.

mic__	rac__	ros__	rid__	bik__
gat__	cak__	nos__	lak__	rak__

- Unjumble the letters to spell the word.

vedri ______________

tega ______________

eibk ______________

iket ______________

caek ______________

reso ______________

Main teaching focus
Phonological awareness: split vowel digraphs.
Vocabulary: Word meanings.

Other teaching focus
Phonemic awareness: Recognising beginning, middle and ending sounds of words.

Teacher's note
Children add 'e' at the end of each word to complete the split digraphs, read the words, then draw a picture to match each word. Then they unjumble the letters to make split digraph words to match the pictures.

Engage Literacy is published in 2013 by Raintree • *A Go-Kart at School*, Level 19. This page may be photocopied for educational use within the purchasing institution.

Pirate Lessons

Level 20 **Fiction** **Word count:** 526 **Text type:** Narrative

HFW introduced: above, act, acting, believe, spoke

HFW consolidated: arrived, idea, learned, practise, really, softly, sounded, through, wear, whispered

Linking text: *Off to the Movies* (non-fiction)

Curriculum link: me/family, school, community, creative play

Phonic awareness: vowel digraphs 'ie', 'er', 'ur'; split vowel digraphs 'a_e', 'o_e'; root word 'all'; suffixes 'ed', 'ing'; double consonants 'gg', 'll', ss', 'dd'

Story summary: Lucy is very happy to be a pirate in the school play, but she doesn't know how a pirate should act. With some help she learns how a pirate walks and talks.

Tuning in

- Talk about pirates. Ask, *What does a pirate look like? What do pirates do? Where do pirates live?*
- Ask, *Have you been in a school play or concert? What is an actor?* Encourage children to act out the movements of a pirate.

Book walk

- Introduce the story. Give each child a copy of the book and discuss the title. Ask children to share what they think the story will be about. Have children make predictions, using the title and cover illustration as prompts. Ask children to think of words that might be in the text.
- Flip through the book, discussing events and illustrations. Promote language that is used throughout the text. Discuss how illustrations help us to read the text. When questioning, use vocabulary from the text.

pages 2–3: Ask, *Who do you think Mrs Crosby has picked to be the pirate in the school play? How does Lucy feel? Who is going to be the pirate Tess on Captain Blood's ship? Do you think Lucy wants to be the best pirate ever?*
pages 4–5: Ask, *Who does Lucy tell about the play when she arrives home? What is Lucy looking for in the dress-up box? What do pirates wear? Could they make an eye-patch? Could Lucy wear the baggy trousers and the old T-shirt? What colour is Mum's favourite scarf? When do you think Lucy learned her lines over and over?*
pages 6–7: Ask, *Where is Lucy's class practising the play? Does it look like Lucy is saying her lines softly or shouting them? Why might Lucy be whispering? Would she be sounding like a pirate?*
pages 8–9: Ask, *Who is Lucy asking to help her act like a pirate? Who is showing her how to walk the plank and fall into the sea? Do you think Mum and Dad are trying to help her, too?*
pages 10–11: Ask, *What movie is Lucy watching? Does it help her to be a pirate? What is Lucy thinking of? What job does Dad's friend Bill do? Would Bill know how to act like a pirate?*
pages 12–13: Ask, *Why has Bill come over? What are the pirate lessons on the piece of paper? How is he walking? How do pirates talk? What do pirates do with their arms? What is Bill showing Lucy? Do you think Lucy is trying hard to be a pirate?*
pages 14–15: Ask, *What has finally arrived? What is Lucy doing as the curtain goes up? How has she walked onto the stage? How would she be talking? What is she doing with her arms? What is she waving above her head? What would everyone in the audience do when Lucy leaves the stage?*
page 16: Ask, *Who comes back onto the stage when the play is over? What is Lucy's family doing? How would Lucy feel? Is she the best pirate ever?*

Reading the text

- Have children read independently. Focus on meaning, structure and visual cues. Support development of reading strategies. Identify areas that challenge children and can be developed into future learning experiences.
- Ask students to relate the text to their own experiences. Ask, *Have you ever been in a school play? What have you had to act as before?*
- Talk about the characters, setting and plot of the text.
- Discuss how this is a narrative text and talk about the orientation, complication and resolution.
- Ask inferential questions such as: *Why might a pirate wear an eye-patch? Why do you think Lucy spoke so softly at the first practice? Why does Mum want Lucy to look after the red scarf? Why isn't Lucy whispering on the big night? Why is Lucy the best pirate ever?*

After reading

Focus on meaning, structure and visual cues that children found difficult while reading. Discuss strategies and provide opportunities for children to consolidate specific skills. For example, if children had difficulty with the word 'family', discuss strategies such as sounding out the phonemes, re-reading, looking at the illustrations or using the sentence content.

Choose from the following activities.

Comprehension

- *Cloze:* As a group, have children retell events of the story. Flip through the text and ask, *What happened in this part of the story?* Copy sentences from the text onto a piece paper, but leave a word out in each sentence. Discuss strategies for working out the missing word. Have children complete **PW 61** (page 103), writing missing words in sentences.
- *Following directions:* On a big piece of paper, draw a large outline of Lucy standing on a stage, holding a flag in her hand. Provide children with coloured pencils. On the board, write instructions, such as 'Colour the stage brown' or 'Draw a pirate hat on Lucy'. Have children read and follow the instructions. Have children follow the instructions on **PW 62** (page 104).

Phonological awareness

- Find 'movie' in the text and talk about the 'ie' vowel digraph at the end. Model the sound that these letters make. Ask children to think of other 'ie' words.
- Find 'now' in the text and talk about the 'ow' vowel digraph. Discuss the sound made by 'ow' in this word. Have children find 'sounded' in the text. Talk about the 'ou' vowel digraph. Discuss how in these words, 'ow' and 'ou' make the same sound. Have children find other 'ou' and 'ow' words in the text and ask them to practise sounding these words.
- Talk about the 'er' in 'ever'. Ask children to model the sound made by these letters. Have them identify and record other 'er' words in the text and underline the 'er'.
- Find 'turn' in the text. Talk about the 'ur' in the word and model the sound these letters make together. Brainstorm and list other 'ur' words.
- Talk about split vowel digraphs and how the first vowel is a long vowel. Find 'came' and 'those' in the text and have children practise sounding them. Ask them to find other words in the text that have split vowel digraphs.
- Find 'all' in the text. Talk about how new words can be made by adding letters to the start of this word. Have children find 'hall'. Ask, *Can you see 'all' in this word?* Cover up the 'h' at the start and have children identify 'all'. Ask, *What other words could we make by putting letters in front of the word 'all'?* (e.g. 'tall', 'ball', 'fall', 'call') Record these words and have children underline 'all' in each one.
- Talk about how the suffix 'ed' can be added to the end of words. Have children find words in the text that end with 'ed' and practise reading them. Talk about how 'ed' on the end of a word means it has already happened (i.e. past tense). Repeat for the 'ing' suffix.
- Have children identify words in the text that have the double consonants 'gg', 'll', 'ss' and 'dd'. Discuss that when there are double letters in a word you only say the sound once. Have children write the words with double consonants from the text, circle the double consonants and sound out the words.

Vocabulary

- *Visual recognition of high-frequency words:* 'above', 'act', 'acting', 'believe', 'spoke'. Ask children to find these words in the text. Ask them to write the words in alphabetical order.
- *Theme words—pirates:* Brainstorm and record words associated with pirates (e.g. 'hat', 'treasure', 'island', 'ship', 'eye-patch'). Encourage children to say these words in a sentence.

Fluency

- Discuss the importance of reading smoothly and without stopping. Demonstrate how to read fluently. Have children practise by reading the text to each other.

Text conventions

- *Commas:* As a group, discuss commas and have children identify the commas in the text. Talk about how readers pause at a comma when they are reading. Model this to children and then have them practise, using the text.
- *Speech marks:* Discuss speech marks. Explain that text between speech marks is what a character is saying. Have children identify speech marks in the text. Turn to pages 8–9 and have children role-play the conversation between Lucy, Ben, Mum and Dad. Repeat with other pages from the text.

Writing

- Ask children to discuss what it would be like to be a pirate. Ask, *What would you do? What would you look like? Where would you live?* Write the sentence starter 'If I was a pirate ...' on the board. Have children finish the sentence and write an imaginative text about being a pirate. Encourage them to include details in their writing and support children in sequencing ideas in their text.

▶ ELL engagement

- As a group, make a pirate mural. Have children paint blue water and a yellow island on a piece of A3 paper to make a background for their mural. Have children colour and cut out the pirate pictures on **PW 63** (page 105). When the paint on the A3 paper is dry, ask children to paste the pictures onto their background. Have children describe the parts of their mural. Focus on enhancing and building children's vocabulary during the activity.

▶ Assessment

- PWs 61, 62 and 63 completed
- Note the child's responses, attempts and reading behaviours before, during and after reading
- Collect work samples, e.g. PW 61 could be kept in the child's portfolio
- Complete Running Record (page 141)

Name: ______________________ Date: ____________

Cloze

- Fill in the missing word in each sentence with a word from the box.
- Read it again to make sure it makes sense!

those	need	black	T-shirt	pirate
best	She	scarf	trousers	said

Lucy could not believe her luck!

Her teacher, Mrs Crosby, had picked her to be a ____________ in the school play.

Lucy was really happy. __________ was going to be Tess — a girl pirate on Captain Blood's ship.

Lucy wanted to be the _________ pirate ever.

"What do pirates wear?" Lucy asked Mum, as she looked through the dress-up box.

"Well," said Mum, "they always wear a _________ eye-patch. We could make one of ____________."

"Look!" said Lucy, pulling out some baggy __________ and a T-shirt.

"We could cut these trousers off, and I could wear this old ____________."

"All you ____________ now," said Mum, "is a red scarf."

Mum came back from her bedroom with her red ____________.

"Please look after it," she ____________.

Main teaching focus
Comprehension: Cloze (with words given).

Other teaching focus
Comprehension: Gaining meaning from text.

Teacher's note
Children fill in the missing word in each sentence using a word from the box. Then they reread the sentence to ensure it makes sense.

Engage Literacy is published in 2013 by Raintree • *Pirate Lessons*, Level 20. This page may be photocopied for educational use within the purchasing institution.

Name: ______________________________ Date: ______________

Following instructions

You will need: coloured pencils

- Read the instructions and make the changes to the picture.

1 Colour the stage **brown.**
2 Draw a **red** scarf on Lucy's head.
3 Colour the flag **black** and **white.**
4 Colour the trees **brown** and **green.**
5 Draw a **black** eye-patch on Lucy.
6 Colour Lucy's baggy trousers **black** and **red.**
7 Colour the curtains **red.**
8 Draw the pirates' gold next to Lucy.

Main teaching focus	**Other teaching focus**	**Teacher's note**
Comprehension: Reading and following directions.	*Comprehension:* Gaining meaning from text.	Children read the sentences and then make the changes to the picture based on the instructions.

Engage Literacy is published in 2013 by Raintree • *Pirate Lessons*, Level 20. This page may be photocopied for educational use within the purchasing institution.

Name: ______________________________ Date: ______________

A pirate picture

You will need: a piece of A3 paper, blue and yellow paint, coloured pencils, scissors, glue

- Paint a yellow island and blue water on the paper.
- Colour the pirate pictures and cut them out.
- Paste the pictures onto the island and water.

Main teaching focus
Oral language: Developing language and vocabulary.

Other teaching focus
Oral language: Retelling an experience.

Teacher's note
Children paint a yellow island and blue water on paper to make a background. Then they colour and cut out the pirate pictures. When the paint is dry, children arrange and paste the pirate pictures onto their background.

Engage Literacy is published in 2013 by Raintree • *Pirate Lessons*, Level 20. This page may be photocopied for educational use within the purchasing institution.

Meeting Milly

Level 20 **Fiction** **Word count:** 512 **Text type:** Narrative

HFW introduced: believe, gently, scratching, they're, trained
HFW consolidated: arrived, closed, idea, raced, really, sound, sounded, yelled
Linking text: *The Senses* (non-fiction)
Curriculum link: me/family, school, animals/pets, community
Phonic awareness: suffixes 'ly', 'ed', 'ing'; vowel digraphs 'ai', 'aw', 'er'; consonant digraph 'qu'; contraction 'couldn't'; syllables
Story summary: Ned is very excited when the puppy, Milly, arrives. But, in the morning when Milly is missing, Ned is very worried. After looking all over the house, Ned finally finds Milly in a special bed!

Tuning in

- Talk about how guide dogs help people. Have children work in pairs, with one child closing their eyes and their partner guiding them around the room. Have children swap roles. Ask, *How was it helpful having someone to guide you around the room?*

Book walk

- Introduce the story. Give each child a copy of the book and discuss the title. Ask children to share what they think the story will be about. Have children make predictions, using the title and cover illustration as prompts. Have children predict whether this is a fiction or a non-fiction text. Ask children to think of words that might be in the text.
- Flip through the book, discussing events and illustrations. Promote language that is used throughout the text. Discuss how illustrations help us to read the text. When questioning, use vocabulary from the text.

pages 2–3: Ask, *Who has come quickly to the door? Who has a big smile on his face and is holding a small puppy? What do you think the puppy's name is? Do you think Ned is excited that Milly has arrived? What do you think Ned and his family are going to be doing if they are puppy raisers?*
pages 4–5: Ask, *Why would they only be keeping Milly for one year? Where would she go after one year? What is Ned thinking about? Does Deb's dog Sultan go everywhere with her? When do you think Ned got the idea about becoming a puppy raiser?*
pages 6–7: Ask, *Where has Ned taken Milly on her first night with the family? Do you think Milly might become the best guide dog ever? Who is yawning? Why do you think Milly would fall asleep quickly? Why was it a big day for Milly?*
pages 8–9: Ask, *Who is Ned going to check on the next morning? What has Ned opened? Where is he peeping? Where is Milly? Who has Ned raced up the stairs to tell that Milly is gone? Is Milly in the laundry?*
pages 10–11: Ask, *Could Milly have got out of the laundry if Dad had closed the door when he went to bed? What is Ned worried about? Could Milly have been dog-napped or do you think she is just somewhere else in the house?*
pages 12–13: Ask, *Who is looking all over the house for Milly? Where is Ned looking? Where is Dad looking? Can they find Milly anywhere? Do you think Ned is getting really worried? Could Milly really be lost?*
pages 14–15: Ask, *What might be going 'Yip! Yip! Yip!'? What room do you think the sound is coming from? Do you think Ned could see Milly when he raced to the laundry? Do you think he could hear her? What does Ned see when he peeks inside the cupboard? What is Milly behind? What is Milly sitting on top of?*
page 16: Ask, *What has Ned gently picked up? Who has jumped up and licked Ned on the cheek? Has Milly found her own special bed? Who is the special puppy?*

Reading the text

- Have children read independently. Focus on meaning, structure and visual cues. Support development of reading strategies. Identify areas that challenge children and can be developed into future learning experiences.
- Ask students to relate the text to their own experiences. Ask, *Have you had a puppy before? Has one of your pets gone missing? Where did you find them?*
- Have children retell the story in their own words and discuss what happened in the beginning, middle and end.
- Ask inferential questions such as: *What things might Ned need to do to look after Milly? Why do you think Deb came to Ned's school? Why is being a puppy raiser an important job? Why was it a big day for Milly? Why was Milly hard to find? Why do you think she went into the cupboard?*

After reading

Focus on meaning, structure and visual cues that children found difficult while reading. Discuss strategies and provide

opportunities for children to consolidate specific skills. For example, if children had difficulty with the word 'arrived', discuss strategies such as sounding out the phonemes, re-reading, looking at the illustrations or using the sentence content.

Choose from the following activities.

Comprehension

- *Sentence match:* Ask children to recall events from the text. Copy sentences from the text on strips of paper. Give children pieces of paper and have them draw pictures to match the sentences on the strips.
  As a group, match the sentences with the pictures and sequence them. Have children complete **PW 64** (page 108), numbering sentences to show their order.
- *Connecting pronouns with nouns:* Copy these sentences onto a piece of paper: 'Ned went quietly downstairs to check on Milly. He opened the door and peeped inside.' Read them and discuss how 'He' refers to 'Ned'. Circle 'Ned' and 'He' in red. Repeat with other sentences, circling connected nouns and pronouns in the same colours.

Phonological awareness

- Talk about the suffixes 'ly' in 'quickly', 'ed' in 'arrived' and 'ing' in 'scratching'. Discuss how these suffixes change the meaning of the words. Ask children to find words in the text with these suffixes.
- Find 'raiser' in the text. Discuss the vowel digraph 'ai' in the middle of the word. Model the sound these letters make together. As a group, make a list of other 'ai' words and have children circle the 'ai' digraph in the words. Repeat for 'aw' in 'yawn'.
- Find 'her' in the text. Discuss the sound made when the letters 'er' are together. Talk about how 'her' can be read by sounding 'h-er'. Have children identify 'er' words in the text and practise reading them. Brainstorm and record other 'er' words.
- Talk about the initial consonant digraph 'qu' at the beginning of 'quietly'. Model the sound that these letters make together. Brainstorm and list other words that begin with 'qu' and have children circle the 'qu' digraph.
- Talk about the contraction 'couldn't'. Write 'could not' and 'couldn't' on the board and discuss how the contraction has an apostrophe instead of the letter 'o'. Ask children to find the contractions in the text.
- Discuss how many words have more than one syllable. Suggest some 2 and 3 syllable words, e.g., 'believe', 'idea', 'scratching', 'quietly'. Ask the children to clap the syllables.

Vocabulary

- *Visual recognition of high-frequency words:* 'believe', 'gently', 'scratching', 'they're', 'trained'. Ask children to find these words in the text. Have children write each of the high-frequency words in a sentence to show they understand their meanings.

Fluency

- Discuss the importance of reading smoothly and without stopping. Demonstrate how to read fluently. Have children practise by reading the text to each other.

Text conventions

- *Features of the front cover:* Look at the front cover and ask children to identify the title, author and illustrator. Explain to children that the author wrote the text and the illustrator drew the pictures. Ask, *What is the title of the text? Who is the author? Who is the illustrator?* Give each child a piece of paper and have them design a new front cover for the text. Ensure they include the title, author and illustrator.
- *Features of the back cover:* As a group, look at the back cover and have children identify the blurb. Discuss how readers can read the blurb to get an idea of what the text will be about. Ask, *Does the blurb match what the text was about?*

Writing

- Brainstorm and record facts about dogs. Look at the illustrations in the text as a prompt for the discussion. As a group, talk about and record facts about what dogs look like, what they do, where they live and what they eat. Have children write a report about dogs, using **PW 65** (page 109) to record their information. Ensure children write multiple facts for each section and support them in using upper-case letters and full stops correctly.

▶ ELL engagement

- Discuss animals that people have as pets. Ask children to talk about pets that they have at home. Ask, *How do you look after your pet? What does your pet look like? Has your pet ever gone missing?* Talk about why people have pets. Ask, *What do you think the most common pet in our class is?* Have children find out by collecting the data using the chart on **PW 66** (page 110). Have children ask each child in the room: 'What pets do you have at home?' Have children record the responses on the chart. As a group, draw a bar graph on a piece of paper to represent the data that the children collected. Talk about how the bar graph makes it easy for us to compare the number of pets that people own. Have children answer the questions at the bottom of the page once they have compared the data.

▶ Assessment

- PWs 64, 65 and 66 completed
- Note the child's responses, attempts and reading behaviours before, during and after reading
- Collect work samples, e.g. PW 64 could be kept in the child's portfolio
- Complete Running Record (page 142)

Name: ______________________ Date: ____________

Matching sentences and pictures

You will need: coloured pencils

- Draw a picture to match each group of sentences.
- Number the boxes to show the order the story events happened in. The first one has been done for you.

Sentences	Picture	Order
Ned went quietly downstairs to check on Milly.		
Ned, Mum and Dad looked all over the house for Milly.		
Inside the cupboard, behind a mop and bucket, was an old basket. And there, sitting on top of some old towels, was Milly.		
Dad had a big smile on his face. He was holding a small puppy.		**1**
Ned gently picked up the basket and took it out of the cupboard.		
"Mum! Dad!" cried Ned, as he raced up the stairs. "Milly is gone! She's not in her bed."		

Main teaching focus
Comprehension: Gaining meaning from text; visualising.

Other teaching focus
Comprehension: Sequencing.

Teacher's note
Children read the sentences and draw pictures next to them to show their meaning. Then they write numbers in the boxes to show the order in which they happened.

Engage Literacy is published in 2013 by Raintree • *Meeting Milly*, Level 20. This page may be photocopied for educational use within the purchasing institution.

Name: ______________________ Date: ______________

Dog report

You will need: coloured pencils

- Write a report about a dog by writing a description of it, what it eats, where it lives and what it likes to do.
- Draw a picture of the dog.

Description
What the dog eats
Where the dog lives
What the dog likes to do
Picture

Main teaching focus
Writing: Writing a report on a familiar topic; using upper-case letters and full stops.

Other teaching focus
Oral language: Discussing facts about dogs.

Teacher's note
Children write a report about a dog by writing sentences in each of the boxes: description, what it eats, where it lives and what it likes to do. Then they draw a picture.

Engage Literacy is published in 2013 by Raintree • *Meeting Milly*, Level 20. This page may be photocopied for educational use within the purchasing institution.

Name: ____________________ Date: ____________

What pets do we have?

- Ask everyone in your class what pets they have at home.
- Keep a tally using the chart and work out the total for each pet.

Pets at home	Tally	Total	Pets at home	Tally	Total
dog			bird		
cat			rabbit		
mouse			turtle		
fish			guinea pig		

Which is the most popular pet? ____________________

Why do you think that pet is popular? ____________________

____

Which is the least popular pet? ____________________

Why do you think that pet is not very popular? ____________________

____

How many pets are there altogether? ____________________

Main teaching focus
Oral language: Developing language and vocabulary.

Other teaching focus
Comprehension: Relating texts to personal experiences.

Teacher's note
Children ask their classmates what pets they have and record their answer in the table, then answer the questions. Children may need help collecting and recording the data and reading the questions.

Engage Literacy is published in 2013 by Raintree • *Meeting Milly*, Level 20. This page may be photocopied for educational use within the purchasing institution.

The Senses

Level 20 **Non-fiction** **Word count:** 506 **Text type:** Discussion

HFW introduced: different, easily, enough, large, loud, person, trained, wonderful, world
HFW consolidated: cover, important, instead, sounds, through, wear
Linking text: *Meeting Milly* (fiction)
Curriculum link: me/family, science
Phonic awareness: split vowel digraphs 'o_e', 'i_e'; vowel digraphs 'or', 'ou', 'ow', 'ai'; consonant digraph 'ph'; syllables; rhyming words
Text summary: Learn about how we use our eyes, ears, mouth, nose and hands to find out about the world. Find out how our senses compare to the senses of animals.

Tuning in

- Draw a large picture of a face and body (with hands) on a piece of paper. Talk about the five senses and have children identify and circle the parts of the body that we use for each sense.

Book walk

- Introduce the text. Give each child a copy of the book and discuss the title. Ask children to share what they think the text will be about. Have children make predictions, using the title and cover picture as prompts. Ask, *What are our senses? What senses are these people using?*
- Flip through the book, discussing events and pictures. Promote language that is used throughout the text. Discuss how pictures help us to read the text. When questioning, use vocabulary from the text.

pages 2–3: Ask, *What parts of our body do we use to find out about the things around us? How do our eyes, ears, mouth, nose and hands help us? What do our senses do?*
pages 4–5: Ask, *What do we use our eyes for? What could we say about the way the elephant, ball and butterfly look? What is a person who can't see called? What do we use our ears for? What could we say about how the drums, flute or the running water sound? What might deaf people wear to help them hear? Why would they use sign language?*
pages 6–7: Ask, *What sense are we using if we use our mouth to taste food and drink? What could we say about how these foods taste? What part of our mouth do we taste food and drink through? Where are our tastebuds?*
pages 8–9: Ask, *What do we use our nose for? What could we say about the smell of the flower, candles and rubbish? What do we use our hands for? How do you think these things feel?*
pages 10–11: Ask, *Do animals have senses? Do you think some animals have better senses than we do? Might some of their senses be not as good as ours? Can cats see well at night when there is little light? Why do you think an owl needs to be able to see 50 to 100 times better than us in dim light?*
pages 12–13: Ask, *Where do we have ears? Why might crickets have ears on their knees? Do you think bats, dogs and dolphins can hear sounds that we can't hear? How do we taste things? What part of their body do flies and butterflies use to taste? Would they taste things when they land on them? Why would worms have tastebuds all over their body?*
pages 14–15: Ask, *Do you think bears, sharks, dogs, moths, snakes and rats have a better sense of smell than we do? What are police dogs trained to use their wonderful sense of smell for? What do cats use their whiskers for? How do our senses help us in different ways? Which of our senses do you think is the most important?*
page 16: Ask, *Where did we see these words in the text? What do these words mean?* Discuss that the glossary shows us the meaning of words that are in the text. Read through the words and talk about what they mean.

Reading the text

- Have children read independently. Focus on meaning, structure and visual cues. Support development of reading strategies. Identify areas that challenge children and can be developed into future learning experiences.
- Ask students to relate the text to their own experiences. Ask, *What senses do you use? What can you see? What can you touch? What things did you taste while you ate your lunch? What things can you smell?*
- Ask inferential questions such as: *Would you be able to taste anything if you didn't have tastebuds? Why do you think cats need to see easily in the dark? What would it be like if we didn't have a sense of touch? Why do you think a baby puts things in their mouth? Would it be good or bad if we tasted things through our feet? Why?*

After reading

Focus on meaning, structure and visual cues that children found difficult while reading. Discuss strategies and provide opportunities for children to consolidate specific skills. For example, if children had difficulty with the word 'tongue', discuss strategies such as sounding out the phonemes, re-reading, looking at the pictures or using the sentence content.

Choose from the following activities.

Comprehension

- *Recall and sorting:* Write 'see', 'smell', 'taste', 'hear' and 'touch' on separate pieces of paper. Ask children to recall facts they learnt from the text about the senses, and as a group, have them record sentences on the appropriate piece of paper. Encourage children to draw pictures on the paper that represent each sense. Have children complete **PW 67** (page 113), sorting and matching pictures and sentences.

Phonological awareness

- Talk about split vowel digraphs and how the first vowel is a long vowel. Find 'nose' and 'white' in the text and have children practise sounding them. Ask them to find other words in the text that have split digraphs.
- Find 'world' in the text and discuss the sound that the letters 'or' make in this word. Talk about how 'world' can be sounded as 'w-or-l-d'. Have children identify 'or' words in the text and practise reading them. Brainstorm and record other 'or' words.
- Talk about the vowel digraph 'ou' in 'mouth'. Discuss the sound made by these letters together. Brainstorm and list other 'ou' words and have children practise sounding them.
- Discuss the vowel digraph 'ow' in 'yellow'. Model the sound that these letters make in this word. Talk about how 'ow' in this word makes a long vowel sound. Ask, *What other words can you think of that have this sound?*
- Find 'trained' in the text and discuss the vowel digraph 'ai'. Ask children to model the sound that these letters make. Talk about how they make a long 'a' sound. Brainstorm other 'ai' words.
- Talk about the consonant digraph 'ph' in 'dolphin'. Discuss how sounding the 'ph' together makes the same sound as the letter 'f'. Ask, *Can you think of any other words that contain 'ph'?*
- As a group, clap the syllables in 'butterflies'. Ask, *How many syllables are in this word?* Discuss the beginning, middle and ending sounds in the word. Count syllables in other words from the text.
- Ask children to identify and read 'white' and 'light'. Discuss how these words rhyme because their ending sounds the same, even though they have different letter patterns. Ask, *Can you think of any other words that rhyme with 'light' and 'white'?* (e.g. 'kite', 'sight', 'fight').

Vocabulary

- *Visual recognition of high-frequency words:* 'different', 'easily', 'enough', 'large', 'loud', 'person', 'trained', 'wonderful', 'world'. Ask children to look up the words in a dictionary and write a sentence for each word.

Fluency

- Discuss the importance of reading smoothly and without stopping. Demonstrate how to read fluently. Have children practise by reading the text to each other.

Text conventions

- *Features of a sentence:* Discuss the features of a sentence and have children identify sentences in the text. Copy sentences from the text onto strips of paper, with the first half of the sentence on one strip and the second half of the sentence on another strip. Have children match the sentence beginnings and endings. Discuss how sentences need to make sense. Encourage children to re-read sentences they have matched to ensure that they make sense. Have children complete **PW 68** (page 114), matching sentence beginnings and endings.

Writing

- Ask children to talk about which sense they think is the most important and why. Write the sentence starter 'I think the most important sense is ...' on the board. Have children finish the sentence and write a text that gives reasons why they think that sense is the most important. Support children in sequencing ideas and developing the argument in their text.

▶ ELL engagement

- Play a 'Senses Guessing Game'. Collect a range of items including: toy car, bag, book, fork, pencil, teddy bear, flower, popcorn, leaf, lollies, pieces of apple and bread, bell, stapler, bouncy ball. Keep the items out of sight. Give each child a blindfold and explain that they are going to use their senses to guess what some items are. Starting with the sense of sight, show children the toy car, bag and book one at a time and have them draw or write what they think they are in the appropriate section of **PW 69** (page 115). Have children put the blindfolds on and touch the fork, pencil and teddy bear. Hide the items and have children take the blindfolds off and draw what they think the items were. Continue so they smell the flower, popcorn and leaf; taste the lollies, apple and bread; listen to the bell, stapler and bouncy ball. Discuss what it was like trying to use their senses. Ask, *Which sense did you find most difficult? How did you work out what the items were?* Show children the items and discuss how accurate their guesses were.

▶ Assessment

- PWs 67, 68 and 69 completed
- Note the child's responses, attempts and reading behaviours before, during and after reading
- Collect work samples, e.g. PW 67 could be kept in the child's portfolio
- Complete Running Record (page 143)

PW 67

Name: ______________________ Date: ____________

Which sense?

You will need: scissors, glue

- Cut out the sentences. Paste them in the table to match the correct sense.

Senses	Sentences
Sight	
Hearing	
Taste	
Smell	
Touch	

We use our mouth.	We can say: "It looks big."
We use our eyes.	We can say: "It tastes sweet."
We can say: "It feels soft."	We use our ears.
We can say: "It sounds soft."	We use our nose.
We use our hands.	We can say: "It smells yucky."

Main teaching focus
Comprehension: Recalling information from the text; sorting and matching text.

Other teaching focus
Comprehension: Comparing and contrasting.

Teacher's note
Children cut out the sentences. Then they match them with the correct sense, and paste them in the appropriate place in the table.

Engage Literacy is published in 2013 by Raintree • *The Senses*, Level 20. This page may be photocopied for educational use within the purchasing institution.

Name: ______________________ Date: ______________

Sentence beginnings and endings

You will need: scissors, glue, a piece of paper

- Cut out the sentence beginnings and endings.
- Match them together so the sentences make sense.
- Paste them on a piece of paper.

Flies and butterflies taste things

Cats use their whiskers to find out if

Did you know that bears, sharks, dogs, moths, snakes and rats

We have ears on the side of our head for hearing

Cats can see in the dark

Police dogs are trained to use

but crickets have their ears on their knees!

very easily when there is little light.

through the little hairs on their feet!

a space is large enough for them to fit into.

their wonderful sense of smell to find things.

all have a much better sense of smell than we do?

Main teaching focus
Features of a sentence: Upper-case letters and ending punctuation.

Other teaching focus
Comprehension: Matching sentence beginnings with sentence endings so the sentences make sense.

Teacher's note
Children cut out the boxes with sentence beginnings and the boxes with sentence endings. They match the beginnings and endings and paste them together on a piece of paper.

Engage Literacy is published in 2013 by Raintree • *The Senses*, Level 20. This page may be photocopied for educational use within the purchasing institution.

Name: ______________________________ Date: _____________

Using your senses

You will need: coloured pencils

- Draw pictures or write in each box to show the things you see, smell, touch, taste and hear.

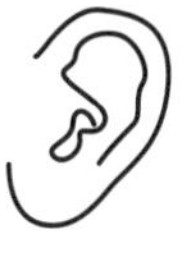

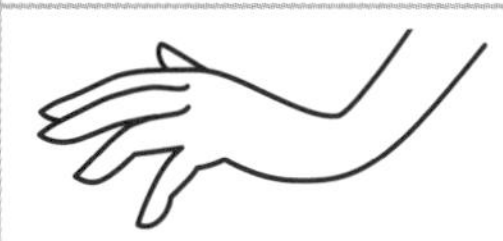

Main teaching focus
Oral language: Developing language and vocabulary.

Other teaching focus
Comprehension: Relating texts to personal experiences.

Teacher's note
Children look at, touch, taste, smell and hear specific items while blindfolded. Then they record what they saw, felt, tasted, smelled and heard by drawing pictures or writing in each box.

Engage Literacy is published in 2013 by Raintree • *The Senses*, Level 20. This page may be photocopied for educational use within the purchasing institution.

Off to the Movies

Level 20 **Non-fiction** **Word count:** 506 **Text type:** Recount

HFW introduced: above, another, being, believe, different, dressed, enough, large, months, wonderful

HFW consolidated: arrived, background, followed, really, wear

Linking text: *Pirate Lessons* (fiction)

Curriculum link: me/family, community

Phonic awareness: vowel digraphs 'or', 'er', 'ir', 'ie', 'ou'; contraction 'couldn't'; suffixes 'es', 's', 'ing'; trigraph 'igh'; consonant digraphs 'ph', 'qu'

Text summary: Read this diary entry to find out what happens on a movie set. Find out how movies are filmed, where actors get their hair and make-up done, and where the costumes are kept.

Tuning in

- Talk about movies. Ask, *What is a movie? How are movies made? What do actors do?* Have some children pretend to be actors and have others pretend to be people filming the movie.

Book walk

- Introduce the text. Give each child a copy of the book and discuss the title. Ask children to share what they think the text will be about. Have children make predictions, using the title and cover illustration as prompts.
- Flip through the book, discussing events and illustrations. Promote language that is used throughout the text. Discuss how illustrations help us to read the text. When questioning, use vocabulary from the text.

pages 2–3: Ask, *What type of text does this look like? Where did the girl go last Friday? Is her big brother, Tom, one of the actors? How will Tom show her what actors do? Do you think the movie is about a family that lived a long time ago? Are there any people dressed for their part in the movie? What are the people riding around in?*
pages 4–5: Ask, *What does the movie set look like? What are the roads made of? What type of buildings are they? Do the buildings look old? Why would they have old buildings if they were just made three months ago?*
pages 6–7: Ask, *What is inside this old shed? Are there lots of rooms? Do they look like rooms you would find in an old house? Would they film the indoor or outdoor parts of the movie here?*
pages 8–9: Ask, *Where did Tom take the girl next? What is kept in this room? Are these clothes the same as the clothes we wear or are they different? What type of dresses do the ladies wear? Who would wear the funny trousers and jackets? What colour dress did she try on?*
pages 10–11: Ask, *What do the actors get done here? Who is sitting near a mirror with bright lights? Do the men and boys wear make-up in a movie? Where does Tom take the girl when she is hungry? What is inside this shed? What did they have for lunch? Does it look yummy?*
pages 12–13: Ask, *Where did they go after lunch? Why would she need to be very quiet in here? Where are the cameras, bright lights and microphones? Do you think sometimes the actors had to go over their lines many times to get them right?*
pages 14–15: Ask, *Which people are the movie extras? Whose job is it to walk around and talk in the background of the movie? What do you think some of these people want to be? Did the girl have a great day with Tom? Do you think she will ask her mum and dad if she can be an extra in a movie? What do you think she wants to be when she is older? Do you think being an actor would be hard work?*
page 16: Ask, *Where did we see these words in the text? What do these words mean?* Discuss that the glossary shows us the meaning of words that are in the text. Read through the words and talk about what they mean.

Reading the text

- Have children read independently. Focus on meaning, structure and visual cues. Support development of reading strategies. Identify areas that challenge children and can be developed into future learning experiences.
- Ask students to relate the text to their own experiences. Ask, *Have you been to a movie set before? Have you seen how people make movies? Have you acted before?*
- Discuss how this is a non-fiction text and how readers can learn about how movies are made.
- Ask inferential questions such as: *Why do the buildings look old if they were only built three months ago? Why do you think the men and boys had to wear make-up? Why does the girl need to be quiet when the movie is being filmed? Why do you think the actors had to keep going over their lines many times? How would being a movie extra be a good place to start if you want to be an actor?*

After reading

Focus on meaning, structure and visual cues that children found difficult while reading. Discuss strategies and provide opportunities for children to consolidate specific skills.

For example, if children had difficulty with the word 'microphones', discuss strategies such as sounding out the phonemes, re-reading, looking at the illustrations or using the sentence content.

Choose from the following activities.

Comprehension

- *Recall:* Have children talk about the different parts of the movie set. On a large piece of paper, draw a map of the different areas of the movie set. As a group, have children draw what was in each of the different areas. Ask, *What did they use this part of the movie set for?* Have children complete **PW 70** (page 118), writing about what happened in each part of the set.

Phonological awareness

- Find 'actor' in the text and discuss the 'or' phoneme in this word. Have children identify 'or' words in the text and practise reading them. Brainstorm and record other 'or' words. Repeat for 'er' in 'brother' and 'ir' in 'dirt'.
- Talk about the vowel digraph 'ie' and model the sound that these letters make together. Find 'movie' in the text and have children identify the 'ie' vowel digraph. Repeat for the 'ou' vowel digraph in 'around'.
- Talk about the contraction 'couldn't'. Write 'could not' and 'couldn't' on the board and discuss how the contraction has an apostrophe instead of the letter 'o'. Ask children to find the contractions in the text.
- Talk about the suffixes 'es' in 'sandwiches', 's' in 'computers' and 'ing' in 'acting'. Discuss how these suffixes change the meaning of the words. Ask children if they can find words in the text with these suffixes.
- Find 'bright' in the text. Ask how many phonemes are in the word (four). Explain that the letters 'igh' make one sound. Write the words 'fight', 'light', 'sight', 'might' on the board and ask the children to sound out the phonemes. Have children complete **PW 71** (page 119).
- As a group, talk about the consonant digraph 'ph' in 'microphone'. Discuss how when the 'ph' is sounded together it makes the same sound as the letter 'f'. Ask, *Can you think of any other words that contain 'ph'?*
- Discuss the consonant digraph 'qu' at the beginning of 'quiet'. Model the sound these letters make together. Brainstorm and record other words that begin with 'qu' and have children underline the 'qu' in each word.

Vocabulary

- *Visual recognition of high-frequency words:* 'above', 'another', 'being', 'believe', 'different', 'dressed', 'enough', 'large', 'months', 'wonderful'. Ask children to find these words in the text.
- *Theme words—movie words:* As a group, brainstorm and list words relating to movies and movie sets.
  Flip through the text and encourage children to use the pictures as a prompt. Turn to the glossary and ask children to identify words that they could add to their list. Discuss the meaning of the words. Have them say the words in sentences to show their understanding. Have children complete the wordsearch on **PW 72** (page 120).

Fluency

- Discuss the importance of reading smoothly and without stopping. Demonstrate how to read fluently. Have children practise by reading the text to each other.

Text conventions

- *Text emphasis/italic font:* Talk about how some words in the text are shown in italics. Discuss that this is because they are words that children might not recognise. Show children how these words are in the glossary and they can find the meaning of them by looking at the glossary on page 16.
- *Text type—recount (diary entry):* Talk about how this text is a diary entry written by a girl recounting her experiences at a movie set. Help children to identify the features of the diary entry in the text.

Writing

- Ask children to write a diary entry recounting a time when they did something really wonderful. Encourage them to provide information about where they went, what they did and who was there, and to explain why it was such a wonderful day. Ask children to use time order words (e.g. 'first', 'then', 'next', 'after', 'later', 'finally') when sequencing ideas in their text. Have children draw a picture to support their writing. Support children in providing details and using adjectives.

▶ ELL engagement

- Talk about 'the olden days'. Ask, *What was it like many years ago?* Show children pictures, books and photos of 'the olden days' and ask them to describe what they see. Discuss how there weren't things that we have today, such as cars, computers and televisions. As a group, compare 'the olden days' with 'today'. Ask, *How would it have been different living then? How would it have been the same?* Record children's ideas on the board. Have them draw a picture of themselves living in the olden days. Ask, *What things would you do?* Focus on developing and enhancing children's language and understandings.

▶ Assessment

- PWs 70, 71 and 72 completed
- Note the child's responses, attempts and reading behaviours before, during and after reading
- Collect work samples, e.g. PW 70 could be kept in the child's portfolio
- Complete Running Record (page 144)

PW 70

Name: ______________________ Date: ______________

The movie set

- Look at each picture and write what happened in that part of the movie set.

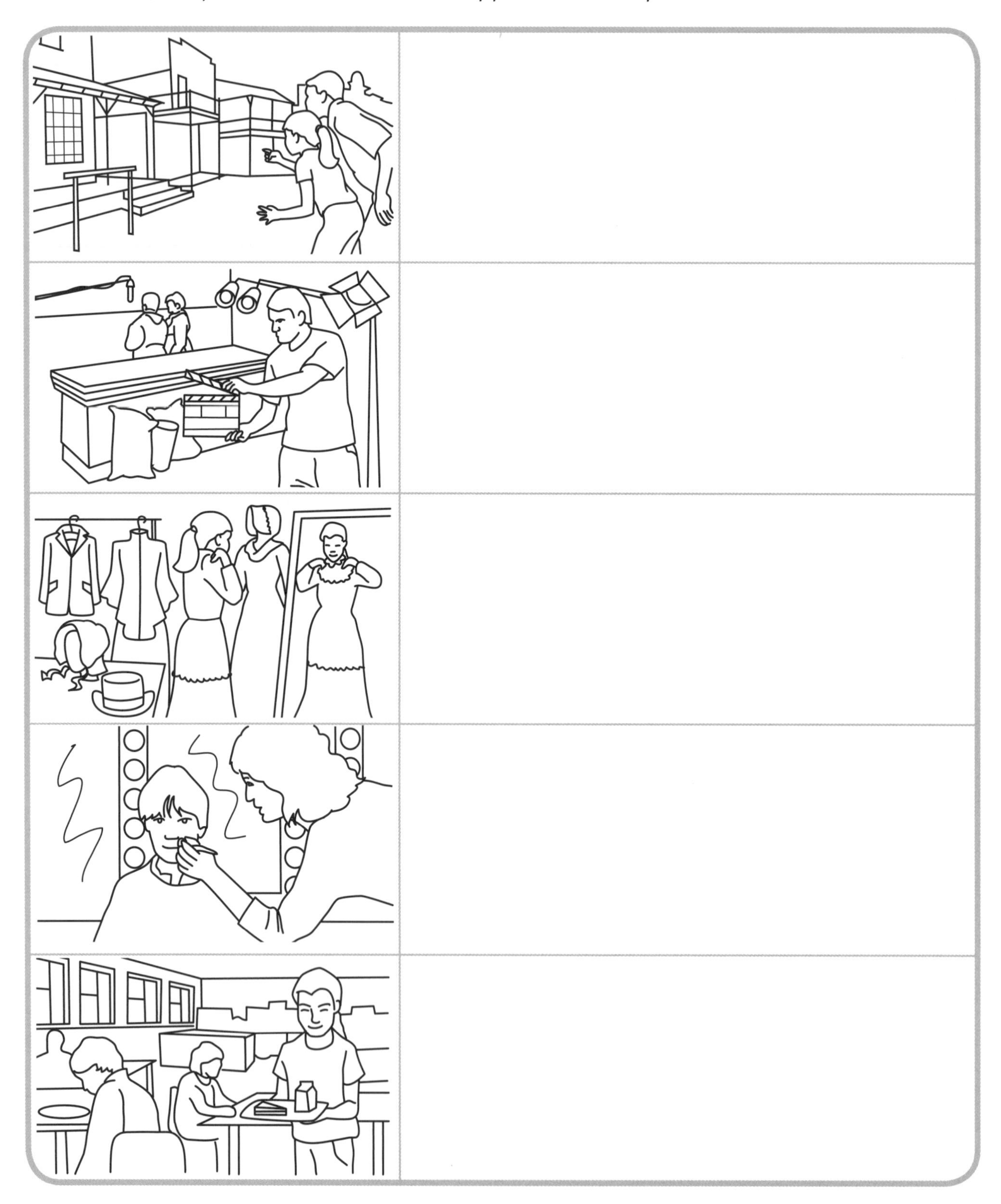

Main teaching focus
Comprehension: Recalling information from a text.

Other teaching focus
Comprehension: Inferring—drawing together information across sentences from the text.

Teacher's note
Children look at the pictures and write sentences explaining what happened in that part of the movie set, referring to the book if necessary.

Engage Literacy is published in 2013 by Raintree • *Off to the Movies*, Level 20. This page may be photocopied for educational use within the purchasing institution.

PW 71

Name: ______________________ Date: ____________

'igh' words

You will need: coloured pencils

- Add 'igh' to each word.
- Write a sentence and draw a picture for each word to show its meaning.

Add 'igh'	Sentence	Picture
br _ _ _ t		
l _ _ _ t		
s _ _ _ t		
fr _ _ _ t		
f _ _ _ t		
n _ _ _ t		
t _ _ _ t		
r _ _ _ t		

Main teaching focus
Phonological awareness: 'igh' trigraph.

Other teaching focus
Writing: Writing simple and complex sentences; spelling patterns.

Teacher's note
Children add 'igh' to each word. Then they write that word in a sentence to show its meaning and draw a picture to match.

Engage Literacy is published in 2013 by Raintree • *Off to the Movies*, Level 20. This page may be photocopied for educational use within the purchasing institution.

Name: ______________________ Date: ____________

Wordsearch

You will need: coloured pencils

- Find the words in the wordsearch. Cross off the word in the panel when you find it.

set	make-up	computers
actor	cameras	mirrors
lights	microphones	horses
indoor	extras	shed
costumes	town	lines

c	o	m	p	u	t	e	r	s	z	b	e
a	m	i	c	r	o	p	h	o	n	e	s
m	x	e	m	q	l	i	g	h	t	s	e
e	i	x	a	w	a	v	s	i	y	p	t
r	n	t	k	c	o	s	t	u	m	e	s
a	d	r	e	h	t	i	h	k	s	a	r
s	o	a	u	o	s	h	e	d	r	k	l
m	o	s	p	r	r	o	d	o	d	e	i
p	r	t	d	s	p	k	t	l	t	u	n
d	j	o	n	e	w	c	z	b	r	p	e
s	q	w	r	s	a	g	x	y	a	u	s
s	a	n	m	i	r	r	o	r	s	v	x

Main teaching focus
Vocabulary: Theme words—movies; word meanings.

Other teaching focus
Writing: Recognising spelling patterns in words.

Teacher's note
Children read the words. Then they find the words in the wordsearch. Words may be hidden vertically, horizontally or diagonally.

Engage Literacy is published in 2013 by Raintree • *Off to the Movies*, Level 20. This page may be photocopied for educational use within the purchasing institution.

Running Record

Name: ______________________ Age: ______ Date: ______________

Text: *Our Baby* Level: *15* Running words: *109*

Summary: ______________________

____

Page no.		Errors	Self-corrections	Reading strategies
2	Rosie looked at Mum.			
	Her tummy was big and round.			
	"When will our baby come?" asked Rosie.			
	"Soon," said Mum.			
4	The next day, Mum's tummy			
	still looked big and round.			
	"When will our baby come?" asked Rosie.			
5	"Soon," said Mum.			
	"Will our baby come today?" said Rosie.			
	"Maybe," smiled Mum.			
	But the baby didn't come.			
6	The next day, Rosie put her hand			
	on Mum's tummy.			
	She rubbed her hand up and down.			
	Then she put her cheek on top.			
	"Hello, baby," she said.			
	But the baby didn't say a thing.			
8	The next morning, when Rosie woke up,			
	Granny was sitting on the sofa.			
	"Hello, Granny," said Rosie.			
	"Where's Mum?"			
	Totals			

Engage Literacy is published in 2013 by Raintree. This page may be photocopied for educational use within the purchasing institution.

Running Record

ENGAGE Literacy

Name: ______________________ Age: ______ Date: ____________

Text: *What is the Matter, Mrs Long?* Level: *15* Running words: *128*

Summary: ____

____

Page no.		Errors	Self-corrections	Reading straegies
2	"Oh, dear!" cried Mrs Long,			
	as she ran into Mr Lee's shop.			
3	"Mrs Long," said Mr Lee.			
	"What is the matter?"			
4	"Well!" said Mrs Long.			
	"I was walking down the street,			
	when I saw a black and yellow tiger			
	running in the park.			
5	Then I saw a big green dinosaur			
	jumping up and down.			
	After that, I saw a little pink fairy			
	with a purple wand."			
6	"Oh, dear!" cried Mr Lee. "Are you ill?"			
	"Oh, yes!" said Mrs Long.			
	"I must be very ill."			
7	"Mrs Long," said Mr Lee. "Come with me.			
	I will take you to the doctor."			
8	So Mr Lee and Mrs Long			
	walked out the door and down the street.			
9	All of a sudden, they saw a black and			
	yellow tiger running in the park.			
	Totals			

Engage Literacy is published in 2013 by Raintree. This page may be photocopied for educational use within the purchasing institution.

Running Record

Name: ______________________ Age: ______ Date: ____________

Text: *Growing Up* Level: *15* Running words: *121*

Summary: ______________________________

____

Page no.		Errors	Self-corrections	Reading straegies
2	Look at this new baby. This baby has just been born. When you were born, you would have looked just like this!			
3	When you were just a little bit older, you could rest on your tummy and lift your head.			
4	This baby can *crawl* and say, "Goo-ga!" Did you say, "Goo-ga" when you were a little baby?			
5	This baby can smile and laugh. She can hold her *bottle*, too.			
6	This baby is one year old. He can walk by himself, and he likes to eat baby food!			
7	Lots of babies can say, "Mumma", "Dadda" and "bubba". What could you say when you were one?			
8	This baby is called a *toddler.* She is two years old. She can jump up and down.			
	Totals			

Engage Literacy is published in 2013 by Raintree. This page may be photocopied fcr educational use within the purchasing institution.

Running Record

ENGAGE Literacy

Name: ______________________ Age: ______ Date: ____________

Text: *Letter to Sam* Level: *15* Running words: *122*

Summary: ____

____

Page no.		Errors	Self-corrections	Reading strategies
2	Dear Sam,			
	Today was my birthday			
	and I had a dress-up party.			
	It was lots of fun.			
	I was sorry that you were sick			
	and could not come.			
	We all missed you!			
	I hope you are better now.			
4	Akio came to the party			
	as a big orange *pumpkin.*			
	He looked so funny.			
	He had green *leaves* on top of his *head*			
	and orange legs.			
6	Karla dressed up as a *mermaid.*			
	She had a long purple *tail* and *shells* in her *hair.*			
7	Everyone laughed at Sally.			
	She dressed up as a *dinosaur.*			
	She had a green face and a long green tail.			
8	My sister and brother dressed up, too.			
	Jill came as a *clown* and Mal dressed up			
	as a big yellow banana.			
	Totals			

Engage Literacy is published in 2013 by Raintree. This page may be photocopied for educational use within the purchasing institution.

Running Record

Name: ______________________ Age: ______ Date: ____________

Text: *Looking for Kate* Level: *16* Running words: *132*

Summary: ______________________

____

Page no.		Errors	Self-corrections	Reading strategies
2	Every morning, before school,			
	Max and Kate would play fetch.			
	"Come on, Max," Kate would say. "Fetch the ball."			
	And every morning, Max would do just that!			
4	One morning, Max woke up with a start.			
	Something was not right.			
	This morning was **not** like the other mornings.			
	Where was Kate?			
5	"Kate!" called Mum from the kitchen.			
	"Hurry up! You're late for school."			
6	Kate moved very fast!			
	She quickly did her hair and ate her breakfast.			
7	She got her lunch from the bench			
	and quickly packed her bag.			
	Then she ran for the door — right past Max!			
8	For the first time ever,			
	Kate did not play fetch with Max.			
	Poor Max! He looked so sad.			
9	"Sorry, Max," called Kate,			
	as she quickly ran out the door.			
	"I can't play fetch with you today."			
	Totals			

Engage Literacy is published in 2013 by Raintree. This page may be photocopied for educational use within the purchasing institution.

Running Record

Name: ______________________ **Age:** ______ **Date:** ____________

Text: *Stuck at the Top* **Level:** *16* **Running words:** *129*

Summary: ____

Page no.		Errors	Self-corrections	Reading strategies
2	Cam and Granny were on the big wheel.			
	Round and round they went.			
	"Look at me!" shouted Cam. "I'm way up here!"			
	Mum waved from down on the ground.			
	The big wheel went round and round.			
4	"Granny!" shouted Cam. "Are you having fun?"			
	"Yes," said Granny.			
	But she didn't look like she was having fun.			
	She looked scared.			
	"Look!" shouted Cam.			
	"We are right at the top.			
	I can see all the way to the sea."			
	Just then, there was an enormous bang,			
	a big crunch and an enormous screeechhh!			
5	The big wheel stopped.			
	Cam and Granny were stuck right at the top!			
6	"Yippee!" shouted Cam.			
	"We are stuck right at the top!"			
	"Oh, no!" cried Granny,			
	taking a careful look over the side.			
	"It's a long way down."			
	Totals			

Engage Literacy is published in 2013 by Raintree. This page may be photocopied for educational use within the purchasing institution.

Running Record

Name: ______________________ **Age:** ______ **Date:** ____________

Text: *Playtime Ball Sports* **Level:** *16* **Running words:** *134*

Summary: ____

Page no.		Errors	Self-corrections	Reading strategies
2	There are lots of ball games that you can play			
	at school.			
	Here are three games for you to try.			
	Anyone can play these games!			
4	To play Down Ball you need			
	two *squares* and a ball.			
	The squares can be marked with *chalk*			
	on the ground.			
	Ask a friend to stand in one square			
	and you can stand in the other square.			
6	When you are ready, *bounce* the ball			
	into your friend's square.			
	Your friend must try to tap the ball back			
	into your square as quickly as they can.			
	You both need to be careful			
	that you only let the ball bounce once.			
7	Down Ball is just like a game of Catchy			
	but you don't *catch* the ball — you tap it.			
	If you miss the ball, you have to start			
	the game again.			
	Totals			

Engage Literacy is published in 2013 by Raintree. This page may be photocopied for educational use within the purchasing institution.

Running Record

Name: ______________________ Age: ______ Date: ____________

Text: *Wheels* Level: *16* Running words: *134*

Summary: ______________________

Page no.		Errors	Self-corrections	Reading strategies
2	A wheel is round like a circle.			
3	Wheels help us to move things			
	from place to place.			
4	To make a wheel move,			
	we have to push or pull it along.			
5	Wheels roll round and round when they move.			
6	Wheels help us to push or to pull things.			
	If you had a very heavy box			
	and you had to push it along the ground,			
	you could not do it.			
7	If the box was in a *wheelbarrow*,			
	or even on a *skateboard*,			
	the wheels would help you to move it.			
8	When we think of wheels,			
	we often think of *cars* and *bicycles*.			
	Cars, bicycles and *motorbikes*			
	all need wheels to move.			
	Trains, *buses*, *tractors* and *aeroplanes*			
	also need wheels to move.			
9	We could not ride a *scooter* or a skateboard			
	if they did not have wheels.			
	Totals			

Engage Literacy is published in 2013 by Raintree. This page may be photocopied for educational use within the purchasing institution.

Running Record

Name: ______________________ Age: ______ Date: ____________

Text: *Wibbly Wobbly Tooth* Level: *17* Running words: *134*

Summary: ____

Page no.		Errors	Self-corrections	Reading strategies
2	Luca had a wibbly wobbly tooth.			
	It went this way and that.			
	It went in and out.			
	Luca could push it all around			
	but he couldn't pull it out.			
4	"Let me take a look," said Dad happily.			
	"I'll pull your tooth out for you."			
	"No thanks, Dad," said Luca.			
	"I'll pull my tooth out when it's ready.			
	And I'll pull it out by **myself**!"			
	"You can't pull it out by yourself," said Dad.			
	"You need my help."			
	"No!" said Luca.			
	"I'll do it by myself when it's ready."			
6	So Luca went on pushing his wibbly wobbly tooth.			
	He pushed it this way and that, and in and out.			
7	The wibbly wobbly tooth felt very wibbly			
	and very wobbly.			
	But it didn't hurt at all!			
8	"Come on, Luca," said Grandma.			
	"What are you waiting for?			
	Totals			

Engage Literacy is published in 2013 by Raintree. This page may be photocopied for educational use within the purchasing institution.

Running Record

Name: ____________ Age: ______ Date: ____________

Text: *Lea Wants a Rabbit* Level: *17* Running words: *136*

Summary: ____________

Page no.		Errors	Self-corrections	Reading strategies
2	Lea wanted a rabbit.			
	"No! No! No!" said Dad.			
	"You can't have a rabbit!"			
4	"Oh, Dad!" said Lea. "Why not?			
	"I'll take good care of it."			
	"We have nowhere to put it," said Dad.			
	"You could make a hutch," said Lea.			
5	"I don't have time," said Dad.			
	"A rabbit is only little," said Lea.			
	"It will not take long to make a little hutch.			
	Oh, please, Dad! Please! Please! Please!"			
6	"Will you take care of it all by yourself			
	and feed it every day?" asked Dad.			
	"Yes!" said Lea. "I will."			
	"Will you clean its hutch			
	and put in fresh straw?" said Dad.			
	"Yes!" said Lea. "I will."			
7	"Well," said Dad, "I'll think about it."			
	"Oh, Dad," said Lea.			
	"Not now!" said Dad. "I have to go to work			
	and you have to go to school."			
	Totals			

Engage Literacy is published in 2013 by Raintree. This page may be photocopied for educational use within the purchasing institution.

Running Record

Name: ____________________ **Age:** ______ **Date:** ____________

Text: *Animals with Fins, Animals with Fur* **Level:** *17* **Running words:** *138*

Summary: ____________________

Page no.		Errors	Self-corrections	Reading strategies
2	Dear Uncle Jarrad,			
	How are you?			
	I'm well, but I have been very busy at school.			
	This week, I did my first *school project.*			
	It was about animals with fins and animals with fur.			
	I want to tell you some of the things			
	that I found out.			
	There are animals that have fins.			
	Fins help them to swim in the water.			
	Dolphins have fins and so do *whales.*			
	Fish have fins and so do *sharks.*			
4	Some fins are little and some fins are big.			
	Little fish have small fins,			
	but a whale has fins that are enormous.			
5	Fins help the animal to swim fast or slow.			
	They help it to swim towards its food,			
	or away from something that is chasing it.			
	Fins can make the animal turn.			
	They also stop it from rolling over in the water.			
	Totals			

Engage Literacy is published in 2013 by Raintree. This page may be photocopied for educational use within the purchasing institution.

Running Record

ENGAGE *Literacy*

Name: ____________________ Age: ______ Date: ____________

Text: *All About Teeth* Level: *17* Running words: *136*

Summary: ____

Page no.		Errors	Self-corrections	Reading strategies
2	Your teeth help you. They help you to eat your food and they help you to talk. Not all teeth look the same. You have sharp teeth called *incisors*. These help you to cut up your food.			
3	You also have teeth with flat tops. These are called *molars*. They help you to chew your food.			
4	You can only see part of your teeth. Under your *gum*, a tooth has a long *root* to keep it in place.			
5	The outside of your tooth is very hard. It is the hardest part of your body. It is called *enamel*. The inside of your tooth is soft. This is called *pulp*.			
6	When you were a tiny baby, your teeth were growing under your gums. When you were a bit older, these teeth started to come out of your gums.			
	Totals			

Engage Literacy is published in 2013 by Raintree. This page may be photocopied for educational use within the purchasing institution.

Running Record

Name: ______________________ Age: ______ Date: ____________

Text: *My Real Name IS Princess* Level: *18* Running words: *142*

Summary: ____

____

Page no.		Errors	Self-corrections	Reading strategies
2	All the children sat on the floor.			
	"Good morning," said the new teacher.			
	"My name is Mrs Kay. What's your name?"			
3	"My name is Bill," said a big boy with red hair.			
	"My name is Lee," said a little girl in a spotty dress.			
4	"And what's your name?" asked Mrs Kay,			
	looking at the little girl at the back of the room.			
	"My name is Princess," said the little girl.			
5	"Oh, no, my dear," smiled Mrs Kay kindly.			
	"What's your **real** name?"			
	"My real name **is** Princess," said Princess.			
	"What a beautiful name!" smiled Mrs Kay.			
	"Do you feel like a princess?"			
	"Sometimes," said Princess sadly.			
6	The children sat at their desks			
	and began their work for the day.			
	Some children listened to stories			
	while others read books with Mrs Kay.			
7	Some children got their books and pencils,			
	and began a story.			
	Totals			

Engage Literacy is published in 2013 by Raintree. This page may be photocopied for educational use within the purchasing institution.

Running Record

ENGAGE Literacy

Name: ______________________ Age: ______ Date: ______________

Text: *Snorkelling with Nana* Level: *18* Running words: *142*

Summary: ____

____

Page no.		Errors	Self-corrections	Reading strategies
2	Gil's Nana and Grandpa lived in a small house by the sea.			
	Grandpa loved to fish and Nana loved to			
	find pretty shells.			
	But what Nana loved to do best of all			
	was to snorkel.			
	Every time Gil came to visit, he asked,			
	"Please, Nana, can you teach me how to snorkel?"			
	And Nana would always say, "When you're a bit older."			
4	When Gil turned eight, he asked again.			
	"Please, Nana," said Gil,			
	"can you teach me how to snorkel?"			
	"Well," smiled Nana, "you're eight now…			
	and I know you're a good swimmer."			
	"Please!" begged Gil.			
	"Okay," laughed Nana. "Let's go!"			
6	Nana, Grandpa and Gil walked down to the beach.			
	When they came to Nana's favourite snorkelling			
	spot, Gil took out a snorkel and some flippers			
	from the bag.			
	While Nana helped Gil to get ready,			
	Grandpa got out his fishing rod.			
	Totals			

Engage Literacy is published in 2013 by Raintree. This page may be photocopied for educational use within the purchasing institution.

Running Record

Name: ______________________ Age: ______ Date: __________

Text: *Happy To Be Me* Level: *18* Running words: *145*

Summary: ____

____

Page no.		Errors	Self-corrections	Reading strategies
2	Dear Amy,			
	I was sorry you were sad at school today.			
	Mr Grant told me you were sad because a girl			
	said you were not good at *dancing*.			
	I think you are good at lots of things.			
	You are good at swimming and *drawing*,			
	and you are the best *piano* player in our class.			
	I know you find dancing hard, but if you keep trying,			
	you **will** be a good dancer.			
4	Some things are hard for me, too — like *maths*.			
	Sometimes, when I can't do maths,			
	I think about all the things I'm good at —			
	like running.			
	I can run as fast as my big brother,			
	and he is the fastest runner in his class.			
	My mum helps me with my maths after school.			
	She says I just have to keep trying until I can do it.			
6	Sometimes I get upset about other things, too.			
		Totals		

Engage Literacy is published in 2013 by Raintree. This page may be photocopied for educational use within the purchasing institution.

Running Record

Name: ____________________ Age: ______ Date: ____________

Text: *Underwater World* Level: *18* Running words: *151*

Summary: ____

____

Page no.		Errors	Self-corrections	Reading strategies
2	Under the sea is a beautiful world			
	full of plants and animals.			
	Some are very small and you			
	have to look carefully to find them.			
3	Others are enormous,			
	such as whales and some *seaweed.*			
4	The ocean is home to lots of fish.			
	Some fish live in warm waters.			
	Others live where the water is cold.			
	Some fish are bright and colourful.			
	Fish can be many *shapes.*			
5	Fish can be big and they can be small.			
	The whale shark is the biggest fish in the ocean.			
	The smallest fish in the ocean is smaller than a *pea.*			
6	Turtles live in this underwater world, too.			
	They have a hard shell.			
	This shell is made up of *bones.*			
	Turtles are under the water for a lot of the time,			
	but they must come up to the top for *air.*			
7	Turtles also spend some time on land,			
	and this is where they lay their eggs.			
	Totals			

Engage Literacy is published in 2013 by Raintree. This page may be photocopied for educational use within the purchasing institution.

Running Record

Name: ______________________ Age: ______ Date: ____________

Text: *Holly's Three White Mice* Level: *19* Running words: *152*

Summary: ____

____

Page no.		Errors	Self-corrections	Reading strategies
2	Holly loved mice.			
	She loved black mice, brown mice and grey mice.			
3	But most of all, Holly loved her three pet white mice.			
	They all lived in a special box in her bedroom.			
4	Every summer, Holly and her family			
	went on an overnight fishing trip.			
	But this summer, Holly didn't want to go.			
	She wanted to stay home with her three white mice.			
	"Mrs Brooks will take care of your mice,"			
	said Dad, smiling at Holly.			
	"She will come over this afternoon			
	and feed them for you."			
5	Holly turned sadly to her three white mice.			
	"You must be very good while I'm away,"			
	she whispered.			
	"You must stay in your box			
	and wait quietly for me to come home."			
6	But Holly's mice didn't wait quietly at all.			
	As soon as Holly had gone, they ran up the side			
	of their box and pushed their way through a tiny			
	hole in the corner.			
	Totals			

Engage Literacy is published in 2013 by Raintree. This page may be photocopied for educational use within the purchasing institution.

Running Record

Name: ______________________ Age: ______ Date: ____________

Text: *Go-Kart Surprise* Level: *19* Running words: *148*

Summary: ____

____

Page no.		Errors	Self-corrections	Reading strategies
2	"How many times do I have to tell you!"			
	said Mick, patting his little brother on the head.			
	"You're too little to race."			
3	Justin gave Mick his crash helmet and gloves.			
	"But it's my birthday next week," he said,			
	"and I'll be eight.			
	I can start racing when I'm eight."			
	Mick just smiled as he put on his helmet and gloves.			
	Then he jumped into his go-kart			
	and zoomed off for a practice lap.			
4	"Mick gets to have all the fun," thought Justin.			
	"All I do is watch **him** and help out."			
	Justin kicked at some stones on the ground,			
	as he slowly walked over to Mum.			
5	"Hello," said Mum. "It's almost race time.			
	How do you think Mick will do today?"			
	Justin didn't say anything.			
6	"You're very quiet," said Mum.			
	"Is everything okay?"			
	"I want to race, too," he said sadly.			
	Mum patted him on the back.			
	Totals			

Engage Literacy is published in 2013 by Raintree. This page may be photocopied for educational use within the purchasing institution.

Running Record

Name: ______________________ Age: ______ Date: ____________

Text: *Mouse Visor* Level: *19* Running words: *155*

Summary: ____

Page no.		Errors	Self-corrections	Reading strategies
2	It is very easy to make a mouse *visor.*			
	It doesn't take very long to make			
	and, when you have made it,			
	you can wear it right away.			
	A visor is like a hat because you can wear			
	it on your head.			
3	To make your mouse visor you will need:			
4	The first thing you need to do is to make			
	the *face* and *ears* of your mouse.			
	To make your mouse's face, cut out a big *shape*			
	from the grey card just like this.			
5	You will need to make it a big shape,			
	so that it fits around your head.			
	This is your mouse's face.			
	It is also the part that goes around your head.			
6	Now cut out two *circles* from the grey card.			
	These two circles will be your mouse's ears.			
	Next, cut out two small circles from the pink card.			
	After you have cut them out,			
	paste them onto the two grey circles.			
	Totals			

Engage Literacy is published in 2013 by Raintree. This page may be photocopied for educational use within the purchasing institution.

Running Record

Name: ____________________ Age: ______ Date: __________

Text: *A Go-Kart at School* Level: *19* Running words: *136*

Summary: ____________________

Page no.		Errors	Self-corrections	Reading strategies
2	Dear Mr Ritter,			
	My name is Clare Ling			
	and I really love go-kart racing.			
	I race my go-kart every weekend.			
	My dad always comes with me.			
	Go-kart racing is lots of fun			
	and it is a great sport.			
3	This letter is to ask you if my dad			
	can bring my go-kart to school.			
	I would like the children in my class to try			
	go-karting, so they can see			
	how much fun it can be.			
4	I started racing go-karts when I was eight years old.			
	My dad is a really good teacher.			
	He tells me everything I need to know			
	about go-kart racing.			
	It's hard at the start but once you learn			
	how to *drive* a go-kart, it's easy.			
	It would be really great if the children in my class			
	could have a ride in my go-kart.			
	Totals			

Engage Literacy is published in 2013 by Raintree. This page may be photocopied for educational use within the purchasing institution.

Running Record

Name: ______________________ **Age:** ______ **Date:** ______________

Text: *Pirate Lessons* **Level:** *20* **Running words:** *147*

Summary: ____

Page no.		Errors	Self-corrections	Reading strategies
2	Lucy could not believe her luck!			
	Her teacher, Mrs Crosby, had picked			
	her to be a pirate in the school play.			
	Lucy was really happy.			
	She was going to be Tess —			
	a girl pirate on Captain Blood's ship.			
	Lucy wanted to be the best pirate ever!			
4	When Lucy arrived home,			
	she told her family all about it.			
	"What do pirates wear?" Lucy asked Mum,			
	as she looked through the dress-up box.			
	"Well," said Mum, "they always wear a black			
	eye-patch. We could make one of those."			
	"Look!" said Lucy, pulling out some			
	baggy trousers and a T-shirt.			
	"We could cut these trousers off,			
	and I could wear this old T-shirt."			
	"All you need now," said Mum, "is a red scarf."			
5	Mum came back from her bedroom			
	with her favourite red scarf.			
	"Please look after it," she said.			
	Totals			

Engage Literacy is published in 2013 by Raintree. This page may be photocopied for educational use within the purchasing institution.

Running Record

Name: ______________________ **Age:** ______ **Date:** ____________

Text: *Meeting Milly* **Level:** *20* **Running words:** *151*

Summary: ____

Page no.		Errors	Self-corrections	Reading strategies
2	"Mum, come quickly!" yelled Ned,			
	as he opened the front door.			
	"They're here!" Dad had a big smile on his face.			
	He was holding a small puppy.			
	"Say hello to Milly," he said.			
	Ned couldn't believe it! Milly had arrived at last.			
	Ned and his family were going to be "puppy raisers".			
4	"She's very sweet," said Mum, scratching Milly's ear.			
	"I wish we could keep her longer than one year."			
	"I know," said Ned, rubbing Milly under the chin.			
	"But Deb said that puppy raisers			
	can only have a puppy for one year.			
	Then the puppy must go away			
	and be trained as a guide dog."			
5	Last year, Deb and her guide dog, Sultan,			
	had come to Ned's school.			
	Deb told the children that Sultan			
	went everywhere with her			
	and that Sultan was her special helper.			
	It was after Deb's visit that Ned			
	had the idea to be a puppy raiser.			
	Totals			

Engage Literacy is published in 2013 by Raintree. This page may be photocopied for educational use within the purchasing institution.

Running Record

Name: ______________________ Age: ______ Date: ____________

Text: *The Senses* Level: *20* Running words: *154*

Summary: ____

____

Page no.		Errors	Self-corrections	Reading strategies
2	When we find out about the things around us			
	we use our eyes, ears, mouth, nose and hands			
	to help us.			
3	Our senses help us to find out about our world.			
4	If we use our eyes, or *sense of sight*,			
	we can look at things around us.			
	We can say:			
	It looks big. It looks round. It looks yellow.			
	When a person can't see, they are called *blind*			
	or *vision-impaired*.			
	Guide dogs help blind people.			
5	If we use our ears, or *sense of hearing*,			
	we can listen to the sounds around us.			
	We can say: It sounds LOUD! It sounds soft.			
	It sounds like water running.			
	Some people are *deaf* or *hearing-impaired*.			
	These people can't hear sounds as others do.			
	People who are deaf wear *hearing aids* or			
	sometimes they use *sign language* to help them.			
6	If we use our mouth, or *sense of taste*,			
	we can taste the food and drink around us.			
	Totals			

Engage Literacy is published in 2013 by Raintree. This page may be photocopied for educational use within the purchasing institution.

Running Record

Name: ______________________ Age: ______ Date: ____________

Text: *Off to the Movies* Level: *20* Running words: *149*

Summary: ______________________

Page no.		Errors	Self-corrections	Reading strategies
2	Dear Diary,			
	Last Friday, I did something really wonderful.			
	I went to a *movie set* with my big brother, Tom.			
	Tom is an *actor* and he has been in three movies.			
	I thought acting was an easy job,			
	so Tom wanted to show me all the things			
	that an actor has to do.			
3	When we arrived at the movie set,			
	there were people everywhere.			
	The movie was about a large family			
	who lived a long time ago.			
	It was at a time when there were no cars or *computers*.			
	Some people were dressed for their part in the movie.			
	I saw people riding around on *horses*,			
	and I even saw a horse and cart.			
4	As I followed Tom around, I couldn't believe it.			
	The movie set looked just like a *town*			
	from a long time ago.			
	The roads were made of dirt			
	and there were lots of *wooden buildings*.			
	Totals			

Engage Literacy is published in 2013 by Raintree. This page may be photocopied for educational use within the purchasing institution.